EAT TWEET

EAT TWEET

A TWITTER COOKBOOK

MAUREEN EVANS

FOREWORD BY FRANK BRUNI

ARTISAN
NEW YORK

To the bluebird on my windowsill, Rhoda Cook,
and her wonderful grandson, my love, Blaine

Published by Artisan
A Division of Workman Publishing Company, Inc.
225 Varick Street
New York, NY 10014-4381
www.artisanbooks.com

Published simultaneously in Canada by Thomas Allen & Son, Limited

Library of Congress Cataloging-in-Publication Data

Evans, Maureen.
Eat tweet / Maureen Evans.
p. cm.
ISBN 978-1-57965-426-9
1. Cookery. I. Title.
TX652.E8948 2010
641.5—dc22 2009049940

Design by Jan Derevjanik
Printed in the USA

3 5 7 9 10 8 6 4 2

CONTENTS

FOREWORD

We have a boundless interest in expanding our kitchen repertoires and learning how to make new dishes; we have very, very limited time. If I had to articulate just a few universal truths about food lovers today, those two would be at or near the top of the list, and of course they are in direct tension with each other: an epicurean paradox, if you will. How to reconcile them? Well, *Eat Tweet* concerns itself with precisely that. You can't boil a recipe down to 140 characters—the Twitter limit, unyielding and unforgiving—if you haven't also boiled it down to the most important ingredients and to a concise sequence of relatively fleet steps. With tweeting comes a kind of fierce discipline and economy. That's as true of gastronomy as it is of grammar.

And that's why it makes so much sense, and has such enormous benefit, for Maureen Evans to play by the rules of Twitter even as she transfers her tweeted recipes to the printed page. With fidelity to the Twitter gods, she is able to put more recipes in less space than perhaps any cookbook has ever accomplished. She saves the reader a great many minutes, her publisher a whole lot of ink, and the forests more than a few trees.

You can roll up your sleeves and make these recipes—that, after all, is the main point of them—or you can in fact appreciate them as objects of unusual semantic and typographical enterprise. They're abbreviation art. The vowels that Maureen drops, the spaces she deletes, her embrace of uppercase, her reversion to lowercase—every decision considered and filtered through the question of whether the map she draws is as succinct as possible yet as deducible as necessary. In recipe after recipe, it is.

Let Ina Garten and Nigella Lawson tell you how to "serve" something. Maureen will tell you how to "srv" it, losing nothing in the process but two superfluous e's. Her No-Knead Bread bakes in a "preheateddutchoven," which you should "Cvr30m@450°; +20m uncvrd." Got that? If you don't, go back and try again. You can crack the code. And you're likely to have a giggle in the process.

Here are recipes that will take you little more than 30 seconds to copy by hand onto a slip of notepaper, tap into your cell phone or—of course—tweet. In that way they are as user-friendly as recipes can be: ez2transport&ez2share.

And lest this collection of them seem spare to the point of stinting, Maureen leavens her pithy prescriptions with the occasional tip on technique. Her minimalism does not come at the expense of utility. "To peel stone fruits," she advises, "score Xs on bottoms, drop briefly in boiling water, then put in ice bath. Remove skins by pulling toward stem." That gives you all the supplementary background you need for a number of recipes, and yet it still hews to the *Eat Tweet* ethos and aesthetic, coming in at under 133 characters, counting the period. Maureen could have used another eight, but is enough of a pro not to need to.

There are cookbooks deemed contemporary by virtue of the techniques they espouse or the way they blend different ethnic traditions. This one is modern in a whole new way. It doesn't consider just what we want to cook and eat. It stands as a testament to how we want to communicate that.

—FRANK BRUNI

INTRODUCTION

I planted the seeds for this book as a Twitter pioneer. My partner, Blaine Cook, was the site's original programmer, so naturally, I signed up out of curiosity. At the start, in the spring of 2006, there were only a handful of users, but our geeky friends were soon adopting Twitter in droves. As a poet and a writer, I asked myself: How can I make sending messages with a maximum of 140 characters more interesting? I felt that life's minutiae had lots of value, but I didn't want to talk about myself; I wanted to convey experiences. I soon hit upon the idea of posting haiku under the handle @maureen, which was both challenging and fun—and a nice distraction from my work.

Blaine and I were living in San Francisco so he could pursue his love of computer programming. I had recently graduated from college and made good on a career goal of my own: I was a self-employed full-time writer. While Blaine was at the office, I was at a desk in our bedroom. As wonderful as it was to be doing exactly what I wanted, I felt somewhat guilty about not having a "real" job. And as I stuffed endless envelopes with carefully crafted poems and short stories and stacked countless rejection letters from publishers, it was difficult to ignore the inherent loneliness and uncertainty of my chosen field. When I got stir-crazy, not only would I tweet, I would charge about town, from library to café, and post office to writers' group. But most often when I needed a break, I cooked.

I'd always found cooking to be relaxing. Growing up in northern British Columbia, a place where hunting, gathering, gardening, and baking are woven into the fabric of daily life, I was surrounded by good cooks, all of whom shared their passion and skill with me. I went fishing with my father, who showed me how to barbecue our catches on a portable camp grill. My mother and I grew vegetables in our yard, and she taught me the elemental techniques necessary to turn them into homestyle suppers. Native American friends of the family demonstrated traditional methods of preparing game and wild berries, fiddleheads, and mushrooms, while our friends with Northern European roots fed me slow-roasted meats in fragrant sauces, and buttery crumb-topped cakes.

Living so far north and in such a remote area, we didn't have a huge variety of ingredients at our disposal—I still remember the romance of my first persimmon sighting when I was a teenager—so to keep things interesting, ingenuity in the kitchen was required. I quickly learned how to improvise, and early on fell away from poring over a recipe's details. Recipes were just guidelines, I realized, and food itself was a creative medium, like poetry, with no hard-and-fast rules about how to make something amazing.

Being in San Francisco only sharpened my love of cooking, and my extemporaneous style. The sheer quality and selection of raw ingredients available all over the city was both mind-boggling and inspiring. The Heart of the City Farmers' Market was not the largest in town, but it soon became my favorite. It sold everything I could want—softly purpled lettuce and bright yellow–flowered choy sum; curling Italian sweet peppers and long hard rails of sugar cane; the darkest green celery and California oranges that sent up groves of scent when I scratched their skins. It also offered great people-watching—Asian grandmas haggling for chilies alongside Castro businessmen; African-American moms buying baskets of strawberries from Latino vendors, who gave out tastes to the kids.

After hours of solitude, I relished the sense of community the market provided. I'd peer into people's bags and wonder what they were going to cook, whether it would be an old favorite or a new dish, and who they would share it with. I was experimenting in the kitchen with many ingredients and cuisines I had never tried before, and guessed that my fellow shoppers were, too. I wanted to ask them about it, but people at a market come and go quickly. Even my friends and I rarely had time to share or talk about what we were cooking, and that seemed unfortunate to me, a sort of undiscovered poetry. Good food, after all, is best enjoyed with others.

All this led me, in October 2007, to start tweeting recipes of everything I made. I pared the preparations down to their essentials to get them to fit the character limit and sent them under my new handle, @cookbook (a name that turned out to be prophetic, though at the time, I just thought it was short and sweet). As with the haiku, it was a fun challenge, but it was also important to me that the recipes would be easy to read and to cook from. Many friends were addicted to Twitter by then, so I suspected they'd take to the format, which they did. They enjoyed the immediacy and convenience of the short form, the excitement of learning unfamiliar recipes, and the sense of assurance it offered; after all, if a recipe could be boiled down to just 140 characters, how hard could it be to execute?

Before I knew it, I was getting recipe requests, blog posts, and replies from three thousand followers. I couldn't believe it—the initial idea of @cookbook was to share my love of food with a few friends, the ones I wished could come to dinner weekly, but who were too busy or too far away. I didn't expect a huge community of online strangers to gather around @cookbook—trying out recipes, discussing and adapting them, and tweeting their own dishes. The conversations I'd longed to have at the farmers' market in San Francisco had become a virtual reality. Through Twitter, I can not only swap recipes and ideas, I can encourage people to share impressions, to try new things, and to be adventurous in the kitchen.

Those are ambitions I maintain today, particularly now that I'm sending tweets to about twenty thousand followers. That number just astounds me, but it is definitely the result of some fortuitous publicity. Blaine and I left San Francisco in 2008 for Belfast, Northern Ireland, where I'd been accepted into a master's program in English at Queen's University. We rented an old stone house smack on the sea. I settled into a routine of writing poetry as a student again, and continued to cook and post tiny recipes in my spare time. Blaine was working on new Web projects.

Life was altogether pretty sleepy until April 2009, when reporter Lawrence Downes wrote an article about @cookbook in *The New York Times*. He noted why I started tweeting recipes, what I enjoyed about food, that it's fun to decode and cook my tweets, and that the lamb tagine he made was a "hit." The icing on the cake was his closing line that using my recipes "re-introduces risk and discovery to cooking, which puts you only a short distance from delight." Suffice it to say that the leap from there to twenty thousand followers and a book deal is 140-character history.

Eat Tweet is the world's first cookbook written entirely in Twitterese (save for the introductions). The abbreviated form might be a little intimidating at first, but with the aid of the glossary, it will soon become like a second language for you, as it has for so many online readers. There's also a demonstration of how to "translate" the recipes also known as twecipes—and helpful tweet-style tips throughout the book, which is organized like a classic reference cookbook. You'll find descriptions of my favorite kitchen tools, a guide to selecting the best seasonal produce, and a section devoted to essential basics, such as condiments, sauces, preserves, and stocks. Many of these recipes are used in later chapters, which include Breads & Savory Pies, Breakfast, Soups & Salads, Noodles & Pastas, Desserts, and Drinks, among others.

The recipes themselves are an eclectic but comprehensive mix collected and filtered from my cookbook shelf, family, friends, Twitter followers, and my travels through more than thirty countries (I love traveling just as much as I love cooking). All are delightfully homey and conveniently no-fuss, yet never boring: a giant, fluffy Finnish pancake with a sweet-tart cherry sauce; spicy Spanish piperada scrambled eggs; lemony-crisp fried artichokes; luscious scalloped potatoes; creamy avocado soup; brightly flavored cilantro prawn noodles; delicate pumpkin ravioli tossed with sage and butter; hearty Guinness stew with cheddar dumplings; a crumb-topped peach crisp that's even better à la mode with honey ice cream; intensely chocolaty devil's cupcakes; a refreshing melon fizz. . . .

Individual technique and taste are part of what make cooking so personal. This cookbook will help you develop your own innate culinary abilities and style, and to approach cooking confidently and with a sense of adventure. Even if you're just learning your way around the kitchen, the minimal instructions allow for a variety of successful implementations and render "perfect" results irrelevant. Instead, "delicious" becomes the objective, and it's a word full of possibility. So please, use this book as though it were your own collection of recipe cards. Write in its margins, jot down tasting notes and adjustments, and share them later online at eat-tweet.com. Join in the *Eat Tweet* community conversation!

Welcome to a new genre of cookbook. Most are linear instruction manuals, but this one is more like a book of maps. And like all maps, it will guide you to your own unique, innumerable experiences. Have fun!

GETTING
STARTED

CHART OF SYMBOLS

SYMBOL	MEANS	EXPLANATION
@	at	indicates temperature or designates a Twitter user name
<	for less than	e.g. "boil<5m" means boil for up to 5 minutes
>	for more than	e.g. "boil>5m" means boil for at least 5 minutes)
&	and	equal measures of ingredients in a step; e.g. "T flr&sug" means 1 tablespoon each of flour and sugar; if before s+p, means T of each
/	and	different measures of ingredients in a step; e.g. "mix c flr/T sug" means mix 1 cup of flour and 1 tablespoon of sugar
,	then	groups actions in a step; e.g. "wash,chop spinach" means wash, then chop the spinach
;	next	separates steps; e.g. "boil3m; drain" means boil for 3 minutes, next drain
+	add	add the next ingredients; also in "s+p," salt and pepper
~	about	approximately; some variation is expected in this step, so use your judgment

DECODING AND CODING RECIPES

All of the recipes in the book yield enough to serve 3 to 4 people, except where otherwise specified. When reading these recipes, you'll find several marked with an Ⓜ. This indicates a master recipe, one that other recipes may be built upon. The variations of the master recipe will be marked with a Ⓥ. Helpful tips for recipes are sprinkled throughout the book. You'll find that the tips most often refer to the recipe that directly follows the tip.

When a recipe name with capital letters appears within another recipe, it refers to a specific recipe in the book. For example, the first step of the recipe for Asparagus Noisette says to "Place Steamed Asparagus in warm dish." Steamed Asparagus appears with initial capital letters because it's a recipe that can be found elsewhere in the book. You'll find the recipe and page number in the index.

Where not indicated, most stovetop dishes may be prepared in a 12-inch skillet or sauté pan or a 6-quart pot, and most baked dishes in a 1½- to 3-quart casserole dish or other common bakeware. When no quantity is indicated, use one of that particular ingredient, such as one garlic clove or one banana. Use your own good judgment, and always adjust seasonings to taste.

HONEY TAGINE
MOROCCO

Brwn lb chopdlamb/2T buttr/
t dryging&turmeric&cinn&s+p;
+2c onion&carrot 9m; +c Stock/
3T honey/9pitdprune.
Cvr~h@400°F.

BECOMES THIS IN A REGULAR FORMAT:

HONEY TAGINE
(FROM MOROCCO)

- Brown 1 pound of chopped lamb with 2 tablespoons of butter and 1 teaspoon each of dried ground ginger, turmeric, cinnamon and salt and pepper.
- Next, add 2 cups each of peeled and chopped onion and carrots and continue to cook for 9 minutes.
- Then add 1 cup of your choice of the master Stock recipes, 3 tablespoons of honey and 9 pitted prunes.
- Bake covered for about 1 hour at 400°F.

SAVORY STRUDEL DOUGH

- Cut together 2 tablespoons of butter with 1 cup each of flour and mashed potato.
- Knead with 2 teaspoons of yeast and 2 tablespoons of warm water.
- Rise for 1 hour.
- On a floured cloth, gently roll out, then pull the dough to a 20-inch square.
- Trim the edges and butter the top.

WOULD BE TWEETED AS:

SAVORY STRUDEL DOUGH

Cut2T buttr/c flr&mashdtater.
Knead+2t yeast/2T warm h2o.
Rise h.
On flrdcloth gently roll,pull20"sq.
Trim,buttr.

TOOLS

Here are the top tools I recommend—they are assets no matter how often you're in the kitchen or what you cook. I've been known to travel with these gadgets.

TIPS

WHEN IT COMES TO POTS AND PANS, THE ENDURANCE OF STAINLESS steel beats nonstick by miles, and is still easy to maintain.

CHECK THE VOLUME OF EVERYDAY DISHES AND YOU'LL ALWAYS HAVE plenty of measuring cups on hand. A typical mug holds 1 cup; a teacup ¾ cup.

ESSENTIAL	EXTRA
One high-quality 10" to 12" chef's knife, kept properly sharp. Dull knives are like dull pencils— not encouraging.	Good paring, butcher and bread knifes.

ESSENTIAL	EXTRA
A 5½-quart, oven-safe, heavy-bottomed sauté pan. A cross between pot and skillet, it can handle everything from soups to gratins.	Oven-safe, heavy-bottomed 8" and 12" skillets and a 3-quart saucepan.
A powerful 9 volt immersion blender (weaker motors burn out easily) is excellent for pureeing sauces and soups right in the pot.	A quality 500-watt stand mixer that supports attachments such as a dough hook, food processor, slicer, food mill, and pasta maker.
The biggest mixing bowl you can find, preferably with a pouring edge and a nonslip base. Everything fits in a huge bowl.	An assortment of sturdy, heat-safe mixing bowls in various sizes; 1- and 2-quart Pyrex measuring cups can do double-duty, too.
A sturdy flat-edge wooden spatula. Its hard edge makes easy work of scraping skillets, stirring soup, and turning food.	A variety of sturdy wooden and/or high-temperature silicone utensils. Keep them at the ready and you'll never miss a beat stove-side.
A flexible slotted metal fish spatula, perfect for flipping everything from delicate fish and eggs to crêpes and pancakes.	A quality metal whisk, tongs, slotted spoon and ladle.
A microplane grater, which easily turns hard cheese, garlic, ginger, zest and chocolate into feathery gratings.	An inexpensive mandoline, such as the Bonriner. It's very helpful when it comes to slicing and julienning fruits and vegetables.

PRODUCE

S easonal produce is beautiful, introducing rhythm and ritual to each year in your kitchen and infusing dishes with unmistakable freshness.

VEGETABLES

MANY OF THESE VARIETIES ARE AVAILABLE YEAR ROUND, BUT are most deliciously expressive at their time of harvest, as indicated in parentheses.

ARTICHOKES (spring and fall) Select any size, with tightly packed, squeaky leaves. Refrigerate unwashed in a plastic bag. Eat within days.

ASPARAGUS (late spring to early summer) Look for firm stems and unbroken tips. Refrigerate standing in some water. Eat that day.

BEANS—BUSH OR POLE (summer) Buy them crisp and evenly colored. Refrigerate unwashed in a plastic bag. Eat within days.

BEETS, AKA BEETROOT (all year; new summer to fall) Buy small to medium, with fresh greens (remove and cook ASAP). Keep in crisper for weeks.

BROCCOLI (all year; peak fall to late spring) Choose tight florets with crisp leaves. Refrigerate wrapped lightly in plastic up to a week.

TIP
TO PREPARE BROCCOLI AND CAULIFLOWER, REMOVE BOTTOM HALF-inch of stem. Cut off remaining stem, peel and slice. Snap off florets to size.

BRUSSELS SPROUTS (fall to mid-winter) Select dark green, tight sprouts. Refrigerate in a plastic bag up to a week.

CABBAGE (all year; new summer to fall) Choose heavy, compact heads. Refrigerate in plastic for weeks (but use Savoy type within a week).

CARROTS (all year; new spring and fall) Choose bright roots. Refrigerate in a bag for weeks, away from apples or pears, which spoil them.

CAULIFLOWER (all year; peak fall to late spring) Choose tight florets with crisp under-leaves. Refrigerate wrapped in plastic up to a week.

CELERIAC, AKA CELERY ROOT (all year; new fall to spring) Choose firm, heavy bulbs. Refrigerate in a plastic bag up to a month.

CELERY (all year; peak summer to fall) Pick heavy bunches with dark leaves. Refrigerate wrapped lightly in plastic for weeks.

CHARD (summer) Choose glossy, medium leaves. Refrigerate in a plastic bag. Eat within days.

TIP WASH AND DRY GREENS SUCH AS LETTUCES AND CHARD BEFORE refrigerating in a plastic bag with a damp paper towel so they're ready when you are.

CHICORIES—ENDIVE, ESCAROLE, RADICCHIO (peak fall and spring) Choose unbruised. Refrigerate in a plastic bag. Best that day.

COLLARDS (all year; peak late fall to spring) Choose smooth leaves. Refrigerate in a plastic bag up to a week or two.

CORN (mid-summer to fall) Choose heavy ears with green husks. Do not refrigerate. Best that day.

TIP TO KERNEL CORN, STAND COBS ON LARGE ENDS AND SLICE DOWN with a sharp knife. To extract sweet juices, scrape cobs with the back of the knife.

CUCUMBERS (summer to fall) Choose unwaxed, glossy fruit. Refrigerate wrapped lightly in plastic up to a week.

EGGPLANT, AKA AUBERGINE (mid-summer to fall) Choose heavy, glossy fruits with fresh stems. Refrigerate in plastic up to a few days.

FAVAS, AKA BROAD BEANS (late spring to early summer) Choose plump pods. Refrigerate in a paper bag up to a week.

TIP
TO SKIN FAVAS FOR MOST RECIPES, SHELL BEANS, THEN BLANCH 1 minute. Use your thumbnail to nick, then pinch off skins.

FENNEL (all year; peak fall to winter) Look for fresh fronds, firm white bulbs and fresh aroma. Refrigerate in the crisper up to a week.

TIP
TO CUT FENNEL FOR MOST RECIPES, REMOVE STEMS AND BRUISED parts, quarter, then slice thin (core only older, tougher bulbs).

KALE (all year; peak fall to winter) Choose medium-sized, crisp leaves. Refrigerate in a plastic bag. Eat within a week.

LEEKS (all year; new late spring to fall) Look for long whites and fresh green tops. Refrigerate wrapped lightly in plastic a week or more.

TIP **TO PREPARE LEEKS, REMOVE ROOTS AND MOST GREEN (USE IN** bouquet garni or stock). Slice lengthwise and swish in cold water to remove any dirt.

ONIONS (all year; harvested late summer) Choose paper-dry, flawless bulbs. Store in a paper bag<50°F for weeks.

TIP **TO DICE AN ONION, TRIM OFF TOP, HALVE TOP TO BOTTOM, THEN** peel. Hold cut-side down by the root, slicing toward it 5 times vertically. Dice.

PEAS (spring to early summer) Choose evenly green, crisp pods. Do not refrigerate. Best that day.

PEPPERS—BELL, SWEET AND HOT (all year; peak mid-summer to fall) Best when light and fragrant. Refrigerate in a plastic bag up to a week.

POTATOES (all year; new fall to winter) Avoid green spots. Refrigerate waxy types up to a week; floury types in a paper bag <50°F for weeks.

TIP **FLOURY POTATOES (IDAHO, RUSSET) ARE BEST BAKED OR FRIED;** waxy potatoes (baby, fingerling) hold up best to boiling.

RADISHES (all year; peak spring to summer) Buy unblemished with crisp greens (remove to store). Refrigerate in a plastic bag up to a week.

RUTABAGAS (all year; new fall to late spring) Choose small bulbs. Keep in the crisper for weeks; use baby tubers sooner.

SPINACH (all year; peak spring and fall) Choose thin stems and medium-size leaves. Refrigerate in a plastic bag. Eat within days.

SQUASH—PUMPKIN, BUTTERNUT, ACORN, ETC. (all year; new in fall) Buy firm and heavy. Store <60°F for weeks or refrigerate more than a month.

TOMATOES (early to late summer) Choose heavy, smooth, fragrant fruit. Store stem-down at room temperature up to several days.

TIP

PEELING TOMATOES PREVENTS SKIN QUILLS IN COOKED DISHES. Score Xs on bottoms, blanch, ice bath then pull off skins. Halve to remove seeds.

TURNIPS (all year; new fall to late spring) Choose small bulbs. Keep in the crisper for weeks; use baby tubers sooner.

YAMS, AKA SWEET POTATOES (all year; new in winter) Choose unbruised and intact—they spoil easily. Store <60°F for weeks (don't refrigerate).

ZUCCHINI, AKA COURGETTE (summer) Choose dark, firm ones heavy for their size. Store in plastic in the crisper up to a week.

FRUITS

TIP VARIETIES COMMON TO NORTH AMERICA AND EUROPE HAVE BEEN included; tropical fruit is less seasonal in availability.

APPLES (all year; new late summer to fall) Choose firm fruit. Refrigerate for weeks away from carrots or pears, which accelerate ripening.

APRICOTS (late spring to mid-summer) Buy ripe—home-ripened can be pasty. Store in a shady spot at room temperature up to a day or two.

TIP AT THE HARVEST'S PEAK, WASH AND AIR-DRY BERRIES, SPREAD AND freeze on baking sheets, then store in bags in the freezer. Scoop out as needed.

BLACKBERRIES, AKA BRAMBLES (summer to fall) Choose firm, tart berries. Refrigerate unwashed in a paper towel–lined container up to a week.

BLUEBERRIES (late spring to mid-summer) Buy plump, unwithered berries. Store in a shady spot at room temperature up to a day or two.

CHERRIES (late spring to mid-summer) Choose clean-smelling fruit on fresh stems. Refrigerate in a paper bag up to a week.

CITRUS—ORANGE, LEMON, GRAPEFRUIT, LIME, POMELO AND BERGAMOT (fall to winter) Buy heavy, unwaxed fruit. Refrigerate loose for weeks.

TIP TO JUICE LEMONS WITHOUT DROPPING SEEDS, TIE HALVES IN DAMP muslin or squeeze halves over your loosely cupped hand.

CURRANTS (late summer to fall) Buy heavy clusters on fresh stems. Refrigerate unwashed in a paper towel–lined container up to a week.

DATES (all year; new late summer to winter) Choose soft, heavy fruit. Refrigerate in a plastic bag for weeks or freeze indefinitely.

FIGS (late spring to fall) Choose plump, unwithered fruit that doesn't smell sour. Refrigerate in a plastic bag. Eat that day.

GRAPES (all year; peak summer to fall) Look for smaller, evenly sized fruit on crisp stems. Refrigerate in a paper bag up to a week.

KIWIS (all year; peak early fall to spring) Choose fruit that gives at the stem end. Refrigerate in a plastic bag up to a couple of weeks.

MELONS (summer to fall) The stem end should give; tastier female fruit bears a circle on the opposite end. Store at about 55°F up to a week.

NECTARINES (late spring to fall) Buy ripe—home-ripened can be dull tasting. Store loose at cool room temperature up to a few days.

PEACHES (late spring to fall) Buy ripe—home-ripened can be dull tasting. Store loose at cool room temperature up to a few days.

PEARS (late summer to fall) They should give near the stem. Refrigerate for weeks away from carrots or apples, which accelerate ripening.

PERSIMMONS, AKA SHARON FRUIT (late summer to mid-winter) Hatcha type should be soft; Fuyu, crisp. Keep in a bag in the crisper up to a week.

PLUMS (mid-spring to fall) Buy ripe with silver-white bloom intact. Refrigerate in a paper bag up to a few days.

PLUOTS (mid-spring to fall) Buy ripe, firm and smooth. Refrigerate in a paper bag up to a few days.

POMEGRANATES (all year; peak mid-summer to winter) Select heavy, large fruit. Store loose in the crisper for weeks.

RASPBERRIES (mid-spring to early fall) Choose fragrant berries. Refrigerate unwashed in a paper towel–lined container up to a few days.

RHUBARB (early spring to fall; the first crop is the most delicate) Choose firm, dark-red stalks. Refrigerate in a plastic bag up to a week.

STRAWBERRIES (spring to early fall) Choose small, fragrant berries. Refrigerate unwashed in a paper towel–lined container up to a few days.

BASICS

Fragrant, exotic spice mixtures you've tailored to taste; big jars of basil-perfumed tomato sauce that turn pasta into a summer-flavored meal at a moment's notice; gem-like preserved cherries or ginger-tinged pear chutney that find their way from breakfast table to cheese plate—these are the secret weapons of your cupboard. Not only will they help keep you inspired in the kitchen, they will help keep you away from the corner take-out place.

In this section, you'll find recipes for those and many other culinary staples, such as stocks, condiments, sauces and marinades, that are indispensable for their simplicity and versatility. Be creative; tinker with and make basics that suit your palate, and apply wherever meat, fish, vegetables and the like need a lashing of flavor.

The most important thing is to start with great ingredients. For example, when preparing tomato sauce, though the pasta you'll eventually serve it on need not be hand cut in Italy, the tomatoes and basil must be the best. The continuous rewards of regularly using top-quality staples will be worth it.

BUTTERS, CREAMS & CHEESES

BEFORE YOU APPROACH ANY NEW RECIPE, ENSURE ALL ingredients and tools are, as French cooks say, *mise en place,* "put in place."

HOMEMADE BUTTER IS WONDERFUL. USE PROMPTLY, OR ADD A dash of salt to store up to a week. Use the resulting cup of buttermilk for baking.

FLAVORED BUTTERS ENLIVEN MEATS, FISH, VEGETABLES, SOUPS and noodles. Make with homemade or store-bought butter; freeze up to 6 months.

Ⓜ BUTTER

Shake2c cold high-quality crm
in 2pt jar~20m until chunky.
Drain(rsv buttermilk),
rinse w ice h2o.
Pack into container.
Yld⅔c.

Ⓥ HERB BUTTER

Cream⅔c buttr/
2T parsly&chive&tarrgn(opt)/
t dijon&garlc.
Form log,wrap,chill.
Slice pats to srv.

BEURRE DE PROVENCE

Grnd2T basil/
2t HerbesdeProvence.
Cream+⅔c buttr.
Form log,wrap,chill.
Slice pats to srv.

Ⓥ MUSTARD BUTTER

Cream⅔c buttr/4T dijon;
slowly+2T lem/s+p.
Form log,wrap,chill.
Slice pats to srv.

Ⓥ GARLIC BUTTER

Cream⅔c buttr/~¼t garlc/
2T parm/½t paprka/s+p.
Form log,wrap,chill.
Slice pats to srv.

Ⓥ ANCHOVY BUTTER

Cream⅔c buttr/
2T drained,mashd
anchovyfillet/2t lem.
Form log,wrap,chill.
Slice pats to srv.

Ⓥ CINNAMON BUTTER

Cream⅔c buttr/2t cinn; slowly
+2T honcy, maple or brsug.
Form log,wrap,chill.
Slice pats to srv.

MOCK CLOTTED CREAM

ENGLAND At room temp,
whip c crm to soft peaks;
beat+⅓c srcrm/T pdrdsug/
¼t lemzest(opt). Srv w
scones/desert.
Yld2c.

CRÈME FRAÎCHE, RICH AND subtly sour, keeps for a week refrigerated. Use where regular cream is called for, or serve as you would sour cream.

CRÈME FRAÎCHE

FRANCE Mix c crm/ 2T buttrmilk in jar; cvr,stand ~8-24h@70°F until thick like srcrm.
Yld c.

CREAM CHEESE

Heat 8c milk/2c buttrmilk 175°F; cool~40m.
When curdled, ladle in wet-muslin–lined sieve. Drain>3h; refrigerate.
Yld2c.

PANEER IS A FRESH CHEESE from India. It's easy to make, grills without melting and can be simmered in Dal or Pumpkin Curry.

PANEER

INDIA Bring8c milk to near boil; offheat~5m+3T lem. Strain in 3lyr muslin; tie tight. Press under hvyplates~h.
Yld½lb.

YOGURT CHEESE IS A LIGHTER alternative to cream cheese and sour cream. It may be substituted for those in recipes or used on baked potatoes.

YOGURT CHEESE

Mound4c (pref greek) yogurt in wet-muslin–lined sieve. Drain>3h; refrigerate.
Yld2c.

CONDIMENTS

TO CAN PEAR AND WINTER CHUTNEY, USE A CLEAN FUNNEL TO fill clean half-pint jars up to 1" from top. Fasten lids; boil as indicated. Cool 24h.

CANNED HOMEMADE CONDIMENTS MAY BE STORED IN A COOL (50°F to 70°F), dark cupboard for up to 2 years. Refrigerate after opening.

TRY SERVING CHUTNEYS AS AN APPETIZER WITH SOME RAITA and toasted Kesra, or store-bought pappadam, available from Indian or Asian grocers.

WINTER CHUTNEY

Chop2c dry apricot/⅓c raisin&
currant&drycherry/4c cider/
c vinegr/T ging&GaramMasala/
s+p.
Simmr~h.
Fill3 8oz jars; boil10m.

HOT OR SWEET—OR BOTH—
chutneys, mustards and
relishes are great with roasted
or boiled meats, sandwiches,
cheese plates and other foods.

TIP

PEAR CHUTNEY

Brwn c onion/¼c oil/T garlc&
ging&GaramMasala; +4c pear/
c celery&date&vinegr/t s+p.
Boil; +lime&zest.
Fill6 8oz jars; boil10m.

HORSERADISH CREAM

ENGLAND Peel,chop,foodproc
3"horseradish/½t vinegr;
beat+c srcrm/2T chive/
T sug/s+p.
Yld c.

A DASH IS ⅛ TEASPOON, OR
about 2 pinches. A pinch is
taken up between thumb and
forefinger. A smidgen is taken
up on one fingertip.

TIP

KETCHUP

Mix¾c tompaste/¼c brsug&
h2o(+as nec)/2T maltvinegr/
¼t grndmustard&cinn&salt/
dash clove&allspice&cayenne.
Chill>4h.
Yld c.

MAYONNAISE

Foodproc2yolk/T lem/½t salt;
while blend@high slowly+
¾c mild olvoil(or other oil)
until thick.
Yld c.

THE EGGS IN MAYONNAISE
and Aioli are not fully cooked.
As such, don't serve to the
elderly, immuno-compromised
or small children.

TIP

AIOLI

Foodproc2yolk&garlc/½t lem
zest(opt)&salt/¼c lem/
2T basil(opt); while
blending@high slowly+
¾c olvoil until thick.
Yld c.

CRANBERRY MUSTARD

Heat t mustardoil to smoke;
cool. Simmr+2c sug&h2o&
cranberry; +3T whl&grnd
mustardseed/t s+p 20m.
Fill4 8oz jars; boil 15m.

GRAIN MUSTARD

Steep6h 3T shallot&ylw&
br mustardseed/⅓c wine
&vinegr/½t salt/dash
turmeric&cayenne(opt).
Puree as desired.
Yld¾c.

SWEET RELISH

Dice,mlx2c cuke/c wtonion
&bellpep; +T coarse salt>2h.
Rinse,drain; +c sug&vinegr/
tceleryseed&mustardseed.
Simmr thick. Yld2c.

TOMATO RELISH

Blend3lb tom/2sweet&hot
chili/3T garlc&soya/
c brsug&rdvinegr.
Boil thick; +mixd ¼c sug/
pkg pectin~m.
Fill5 8oz jars; boil15m.

THIS NOUVELLE CUISINE
preparation, created by Guy
Martin of Paris' Grand Véfour,
is ephemeral with cheese or
tossed with cold tagliatelle.

TIP

VANILLA ZUCCHINI RELISH

Trim,ribbon-cut6sm zuke/
3T ging.
Mix c sug/½vanilbean/
T lemzest.
Lyr4x; cvr w 2lem.
Chill>16h.
Yld3c.

APPLE SAUCE

Peel,core,chop7apple;
+½c h2o. Cvr,simmr,stir
occas~10m; +T lem&
sug(opt)/¼t cinn&clove.
Yld2c.

CRANBERRY SAUCE

Simmr c h2o/cinnstick/
3whlclove/cardamompod/strip
lem&orange zest/2c cranberry
to burst; +½c sug(+to taste).
Yld c.

TIP CHOKA AND LECSÓ ARE SPICY stewed vegetables used as condiments on meats, rice and eggs; Harissa and Romesco work similarly, so experiment.

CHOKA

TRINIDAD Chop,cvr
2eggplant&tom h@375°F.
Foodproc flesh+wtonion.
Heat T garlc/⅛t nutmeg&cinn
&chili/¼c oil; mix+roast veg.
Yld2c.

TIP INCLUDE A VARIETY OF PEPPERS in Lecsó for rich flavor and color: Hungarian, Italian, banana, Anaheim and mixed bell peppers work well.

LECSÓ

HUNGARY Sauté3T lard
(or buttr)/onion; +T garlc/
4c multi-color sweet-hot pep.
Simmr15m+2T paprka/
2c tom/s+p.
Yld3c.

TIP FOR DETAILS ON HOW TO prepare the bell pepper for the Romesco sauce, see the Roasted Peppers recipe.

ROMESCO

SPAIN Charbroil,peel,
seed rdbellpep.
Puree+pce toast/4tom/
⅓c hazelnut&vinegr&olvoil/
T garlc/chili&s+p to taste.
Yld2c.

HARISSA

MOROCCO Soak12drychili/
hot h2o to cvr~30m.
Grnd+T olvoil&chili h2o(+as
nec)/4garlc/2t coriandr&
cumin&caraway/½t salt.
Yld c.

THESE PICKLES ARE
fermented like sauerkraut.
The zip bag serves to force
them beneath the brine.
Harmless fuzzy mold should
be skimmed off.

TIP

DILL PICKLES

Put¼c picklingspice&dill&garlc/
½c wtvinegr&coarsesalt/3lb
sm cuke/5c h2o in gallonjar.
Top w h2o in zipbag.
Skim 1/d~3wk@70°F.

ROASTED EGGPLANT

Slice½"circles; +t salt.
Drain20m.
Rinse,pat dry well.
Coat w olvoil + pep.
Broil3m/side@med-hlgh.

WHEN YOU ROAST GARLIC, DO
many bulbs at once; they're
luscious hot with crackers and
lend savoriness when added to
pastas, soups and stews.

TIP

ROASTED GARLIC

Cut½" off bulbtop to expose
clvs; +½t olvoil~m to absorb;
+½t olvoil.
Cvr w foil,roast~h@350°F.

ROASTED PEPPERS

Turn often under broiler until
blackened. Cool in paper bag,
then pull off skin and remove
stem, inner ribs and seeds.

OVEN-ROASTED DRIED TOMATOES

Halve lb sm plum or cherry
tom; dust w t pdrdsug&oreg or
thyme(opt)/s+p. 2h@200°F.

MARINADES & MOPS

TIP **MARINATE VEGETABLES, TOFU, POULTRY AND MEAT IN THE** refrigerator for up to 8 hours, but most fish is best marinated for less than an hour.

CHERMOULA
MOROCCO Grnd T garlc/
t salt&cumin&paprka&dryging/
c cilantro&parsly; +3lem/
¼c olvoil/¼-½t cayenne.
Yld c.

LEMON-HERB MARINADE
Mix⅔c oil&lem/1⅓c wtwine/
2slicedlem&onion&celery/
2sprg parsly&bay&thyme&dill.
Yld 3c. Marinates~2lb food.

WHITE-WINE MARINADE
Mix3c wtwine/c pineapjuice&
oj/lem/shallot&bay/5cracked
pepcorn/¼t ging&lemzest.
Yld 5c. Marinates~3lb food.

ESPRESSO BBQ SAUCE
Simmr¾c ketchup/
3T vinegr&espresso&brsug
&oil/T worces/2t celery
seed&garlc/dash cayenne.
Yld c. Cvr~2lb food.

TIP

TO AVOID BURNING SWEET
and spicy glazes and barbecue
sauces, apply them twice near
the end of grilling.

MUSTARD BBQ SAUCE

Simmr⅓c vinegr&mustard
&shallot/2T tompaste/
2t paprka&garlc/t salt&
grndmustard/¼t pep
~20m@low.
Yld c. Cvr~2lb food.

TIP

THIS MILD MISO SAUCE, FROM
my favorite restaurant, San
Francisco's Minako, is great
on grilled eggplant, sweet
potatoes and scallops.

YOKO KONDO'S
DENGAKU SAUCE

JAPAN Mix4oz brmiso/
⅓c sug/¼c Dashi/
2½t sake/t mirin.
Yld c. Cvr~2lb food.

MARMALADE GLAZE

Mix⅓c lem&oil&marmalade/
T rosemry&garlc/s+p.
Finish glazed/grilled food
w ¼c h2o-thinned
marmalade.
Yld c. Cvr~2lb food.

MAPLE PEACH GLAZE

Peel,chop lb peach.
Cvr,simmr+5T maple&h2o;
+T vinegr&horseradish/t ging/
½t s+p~10m until thick.
Yld c. Cvr~2lb food.

PRESERVES

TIPS

TO CAN THE FOLLOWING ITEMS, USE A CLEAN FUNNEL TO FILL clean half-pint jars up to 1" from top. Fasten lids; boil as indicated. Cool 24h.

CANNED HOMEMADE PRESERVES MAY BE STORED IN A COOL (50°F to 70°F), dark cupboard for up to 2 years. Refrigerate after opening.

TO TEST THAT JAM HAS SET, DOLLOP SOME ONTO A CHILLED plate and run your finger through it. If the trail doesn't close up, it's ready.

APPLE BUTTER

Chop3lb apple.
Boil soft+2c h2o&applejuice;
sieve.
Simmr thick+⅓c sug&lem/
½t cinn/¼t allspice&clove.
Fill4 8oz jars; boil15m.

BLACKBERRY JAM

Crush4c blackberry(some
unripe helps set); boil+
¼c lem/can frozen juice;
+c sug.
Boil hard to set.
Fill4 8oz jars; boil15m.

PEACH PASSION JAM

Boil c passionfruit/4c peach/
¼c lem/can frozen juice;
+mixd c sug/pkg pectin.
Boil hard to set.
Fill4 8oz jars; boil15m.

GINGER BERRY JAM

Boil4c berry/T ging/can frozen
rdgrapejuice/¼c lem; +mixd
c sug/pkg pectin.
Boil hard to set.
Fill4 8oz jars; boil15m.

LEMON CURD

Zest,juice lb meyer or reg lem.
Simmr in bainmarie+2c sug/
c buttr; whisk+5btnegg.
Stir20m@low to set.
Fill5 8oz jars; boil10m.

STRAWBERRY, MINT & PEPPER JAM

Crush5c strawberry.
Boil+¼t pep/¼c lem&mint/
can frozen juice; +mixd
c sug/pkg pectin.
Fill4 8oz jars; boil15m.

FOR CLEARER MARMALADE,
choose citrus with thin pith.
Slice as thinly as possible.
Soaking draws pectins from
peel and seeds to set the jam.

TIP

MEYER LEMON MARMALADE

Slice2lb meyerlem; +h2o to
yld4c/seeds in muslin>8h.
Simmr thick+3c sug
~½h@low.
Remove seeds, fill4 8oz jars;
boil15m.

ORANGE MARMALADE

Slice2lb orange; +h2o to
yld4c/seeds in muslin>8h.
Simmr+3c sug~h@low.
Fill4 8oz jars; boil15m.

HARVESTED IN CALIFORNIA IN
winter, bergamot is an
aromatic citrus used in Earl
Grey tea. You may sub a lime
or teaspoon of dry lavender.

TIP

BLOOD ORANGE BERGAMOT MARMALADE

Slice2lb bloodorange;
+h2o to yld4c>8h.
Simmr+3c sug~h@low;
+slicedbergamot 2m.
Fill4 8oz jars; boil15m.

TO CAN THE FOLLOWING ITEMS,
pack into clean pint jars.
Add hot, reboiled syrup to 1"
from top. Fasten lids; boil as
indicated. Cool 24h.

TIP

Ⓜ PRESERVED CHERRIES

Boil4c sug/c h2o/
3lb pitdcherry. Cool3h;
fill4 16oz jars w fruit.
Boil syrup+2c applejuice/
lem>220°F.
Fill jars; boil10m.

TO PEEL STONE FRUITS, score Xs on bottoms, drop briefly in boiling water, then put in ice bath. Remove skins by pulling toward stem.

LIQUOR-PRESERVED FRUITS improve with time and are simply divine on ice cream. Store for up to 2 years.

Ⓥ PRESERVED STONE FRUITS

Halve,pit3lb peeld peach or apricot.
Proceed as for Preserved Cherries, but simmr very gently.

Ⓜ BRANDIED CHERRIES

Simmr c h2o&sug/staranise &cinnstick 10m; +2lb pitd cherry 5m@low.
Fill5 8oz jars; +½e brandy &syrup to cvr; boil5m.

Ⓥ BRANDIED STONE FRUITS

Halve,pit2lb peeld peach, apricot or plum(no need to peel plums).
Proceed as for Brandied Cherries.

WHISKY APPLES

Boil2c h2o&sug;
⊢4c tartapple/cinnstick.
Simmr4m; rmv apple to 4 8oz jars.
Boil syrup 5m; +½c whisky.
Fill jars; boil5m.

SAUCES

TIPS

TO PREPARE A SIMPLE SAUCE AFTER BROWNING MEAT, SAUTÉ shallot and garlic in the pan. Add a cup of stock; reduce. Whisk in butter, lemon, s+p.

THE EGGS IN SOME OF THESE SAUCES ARE NOT FULLY COOKED. As such, don't serve to the elderly, immuno-compromised, or small children.

Ⓜ BÉARNAISE SAUCE

Sauté T shallot/t tarrgn/
s+p/3T vinegr~3m.
Cool; +2btn yolk/T h2o.
Whisk thick@low; slowly+
½c buttr.
Yld¾c.

Ⓥ CHORON SAUCE

Stir½c sieved TomSauce or mixd ¼c tompaste&crm into Béarnaise.

Ⓜ BÉCHAMEL

Mlt2T buttr@med-high;
+2T flr.
Whisk@low to brwn.
Slowly whisk+c milk to
desired thickness; s+p.
Cvr immed.
Yld c.

Ⓥ BROWN SAUCE

Use BeefStock/pinch dry
thyme in place of milk in
Béchamel.

Ⓥ CHEESE SAUCE

Stir in c crumbled or
grtdcheese(eg swiss/blue/
cheddar)/¼t dijon/dash paprka
(opt)just before Béchamel is
thickened to taste.

Ⓥ ONION SAUCE

Stir c caramelized onion/
½c grtdcheese(opt)/dash
cayenne&drythyme(opt)after
thickening Béchamel.

Ⓥ VELOUTÉ

Use Chicken or Vegetable
Scrap Stock in place of milk
in Béchamel.

HOLLANDAISE

Whisk3yolk/2T h2o/
dash salt @low until foamy.
Offheat slowly+ ⅓c softbuttr.
Whisk thick@low; +t lem/
dash cayenne(opt).
Yld¾c.

MINT HOLLANDAISE

Mlt⅓c butter&mint;
rmv mint,cool buttr.
Whisk3yolk/2T h2o/s+p
@low until foamy; slowly
whisk thick+buttr; +T lem.
Yld¾c.

@AARONOFMONTREAL'S PESTO

Foodproc or mortar grnd
t salt/2garlc/2T pinenut/
2c basil/½c olvoil&parm.
Yld¾c.
Use 2T/srvg(+T hot h2o
to thin).

ASIAN PESTO

Grnd T garlc&ging/
c cilantro&thaibasil/
½c cashew/T soya; slowly+
2T lime&oil&sesoil.
Yld ¾c. Use 2T/srvg(+T hot
h2o to thin).

TIP

PESTO PACKS A PUNCH ON
vegetables and soup, pizza
and pasta. Freeze in ice cube
trays, then store in a freezer
bag for up to a few months.

ASPARAGUS PESTO

Blanch ½lb aspargusstem
~3m. Grnd+½c spinach&
pinenut&parm/2T olvoil
&lem/t garlc/s+p.
Yld c. Use 3T/srvg(+T hot h2o
to thin).

TOMATO PESTO

Soak8sundriedtom/hot h2o.
Grnd+T garlc/t salt/2c basil;
+½c olvoil&parm/¼c
tompaste. Yld c. Use 2T/
srvg(+T hot h2o to thin).

TIP

CANNED TOMATOES LEND
summer flavor all year, and
can sub for fresh tomatoes in
cooked recipes. Don't omit
lemon; it's there for food
safety.

CANNED TOMATOES

Chop15tom/¼c basil(opt).
Cvr,simmr10m@med.
Blend,bring to boil.
Funnel+T lem e into 3-4pt
jars; boil15m.

TIP

USE CANNED TOMATOES OR
fresh ones (skin/seeds optional)
to prepare these sauces, any
of which may be used where a
recipe calls for TomSauce.

TOMATO SAUCE

Sauté2onion/T garlc&olvoil
&buttr. Deglaze+c rdwine.
Simmr5m; +4c tom/
2T ItalianMix/s+p.
Simmr½cvrd~h.
Sieve(opt).
Yld6c.

HOT ROSEMARY TOMATO SAUCE

Mince T rosemry&garlc
&chili. Sauté+T olvoil;
+4c tom. Cvr30m@low;
+mixd t flr/T milk 5m; s+p.
Yld2c.

LENTIL TOMATO SAUCE

Sauté T oil&garlc&Italian
Mix; +onion 7m; +2c tom&
Stock/½c rdlentil/
3T tompaste. Cvr20m.
Sieve;+⅓c crm(opt)/s+p.
Yld2c.

ROASTED TOMATO SAUCE

Chop,mix3lb tom/onion/
sprgoreg/⅓c olvoil&
whlgarlc/s+p.
Partly cvr in bkgdish
~h@375°F
Sieve(opt); +3 l tompaste.
Yld2c.

TIP

AVGOLEMONO AND COCONUT
Sauce are delicate accompani-
ments to fish, chicken and
rice; the latter suits spicy
foods, such as Pumpkin Curry.

AVGOLEMONO

GREECE Beat2egg/⅓c lem.
Whisk+½c hot Stock;
+another ½c hot Stock.
Cvr5m.
Yld c.

COCONUT SAUCE

THAI Foodproc can cocont/
shallot/2garlc/2T oil&fresh
inner lemongrass/½c peanut/
chili&s+p to taste.
Chill2h.
Yld2c.

CITRUS SAUCE

Brwn3T shallot&oil.
Simmr5m+½c ricewine&
Dashi/t garlc&lem&lime
zest/3T soya; +t sesoil/
2T lem&lime.
Yld c.

TIP

TAMARIND IS AN ESSENTIAL flavor in Thai cooking. Buy as pulp or in blocks (to turn block into pulp, soak, mix and sieve with 4c hot h2o).

TIP

USE THIS BEGUILING CURRY from Vancouver's Vij's restaurant on many vegetables and meats. It's also essential for Vikram Vij's Lamb Chops.

STIR-FRY SAUCE

THAI Mix½c tamarind pulp&fishsauce(or soya)/ ⅓c brsug. Simmr5m@ med-low; +t chili&garlc. Enough for 2 PadThai recipes.

VIKRAM VIJ'S FENUGREEK CURRY

Sauté3T oil&garlc; +t turmeric; +mixd 4c crm/ ¼c lem/T fenugreekleaf& salt/t paprka/cayenne. Simmr5m.

Ⓜ GRAVY

Skim,rsv fat from roastpan; deglaze+4c Stock. Boil,strain; +2T wtwine,rsv. Brwn¼c rsvdfat&flr. Slowly whisk in rsvdstock; s+p.

Ⓥ FANCY GRAVY

Chop,place carrot&celery &onion under roast; rmv to deglaze pan. Mash,sieve into rsvdstock w the wtwine when making Gravy.

SEASONINGS

ADD FRESH HERBS AT THE END OF COOKING, DRY AT THE START.
Generally, a tablespoon of fresh herbs equals a teaspoon of dry.

DRY SEASONINGS IMPROVE WITH HEAT. DRAW A BAY LEAF
across a flame to bring its fragrance to life, and pan-toast seeds.

KEPT SEALED IN A COOL, DARK PLACE (NOT BESIDE THE STOVE),
whole spices keep 4 years, ground spices 2, and dry herbs 1.

FRESH BOUQUET GARNI (BQTGRNI)

Per bundle, wrap3sprg
thyme&parsly/celerytop&
tarrgn/garlc&bay in 6"leek
green; tie well w string.
Freeze.

DRY BOUQUET GARNI (BQTGRNI)

Per bundle, tie2bay/½t dry
thyme&tarrgn&marjoram/
¼t celeryseed&allspice into
muslin.
Store airtight.

TIP

CREOLE SPICE IS A MIX OF seasonings similar to chili powder, with the distinctive addition of the thickener filé, ground sassafras leaves.

CREOLE SPICE

Mix3T dry basil&thyme&
papkra/2T cayenne/
T filé&chili pdr.
Store airtight.

CURRY POWDER

INDIA Stir in skillet@low until fragrant 2T whl cumin&
cardamom&coriandr&turmeric/
t dry chili&dryging.
Grnd.
Store airtight.

TIP

FIVE-SPICE POWDER encompasses all the flavors of Chinese cuisine: sweet, sour, bitter, pungent and salty.

FIVE-SPICE POWDER

Stir@low until fragrant
2t szechuan pepcorn:
foodproc+8staranise/
T fennelseed; +grnd T cinn/
½t clove.
Store airtight.

GARAM MASALA

INDIA Stir in skillet@low until fragrant ½t whl clove
&pep&cardamom&cinn
&coriandr/3T whlcumin/
¼t nutmeg.
Grnd.
Store airtight.

HERBES DE PROVENCE

FRANCE Grnd T dry basil
&marjoram&savory&thyme/
bay/t fennelseed&lavender
(opt). Store airtight.

ITALIAN MIX

Grnd2T dry basil&
marjoram&oreg/2t dry
rosemry&thyme&sage&
chili/½t fennelseed&celery
seed(opt).
Store airtight.

SAVORY SPICE

Grnd2T dry sage/T dry
thyme&marjoram&savory/
t s+p&lemzest/½t turmeric
&bay/¼t nutmeg&clove.
Store airtight.

SPICE MIXES MAY BE CUSTOM-
tailored. Savory Spice suits
poultry, gravy and vegetables;
Sweet Spice adds warmth to
baked goods and desserts.

TIP

SWEET SPICE

Stir in skillet@low until
fragrant 2T dry ging&cinn/
T nutmeg/t clove/
½t wtpep&cardamom.
Grnd.
Store airtight.

STOCKS

POACH MEAT OR FISH IN COURT BOUILLON, THEN USE THE poaching broth to make a sauce. Reduce a cup to half; whisk in butter and lemon to taste.

TO MAKE STOCK, USE BEEF SHIN/SHANK/MARROW/RIB BONES; chicken or turkey carcass/wingtips/necks/backs; non-oily fish heads/backs.

COURT BOUILLON

Cvr,simmr30m c wtwine/
5c h2o/⅓c vinegr/2onion
&carrot&celery&bay/
2t salt/12pepcorn.
Strain.
Yld4c.

BEEF STOCK

Boil lb bones/6c h2o/
carrot&onion/t salt&
pepcorn/BqtGrni; skim.
Cvr5h@low.
Strain,cool,skim.
Yld4c.

CHICKEN STOCK

Boil lb bones/6c h2o/t salt
&pepcorn/carrot&celery/
BqtGrni; skim.
Cvr3h@low.
Strain,cool,skim.
Yld4c.

THIS TURKEY STOCK IS
perfect for making turkey
stuffing and gravy because
it can be prepared before or
while the bird is roasting.

TIP

LIGHT TURKEY STOCK

Boil10c h2o/rinsed turkey
giblet&neck/2 carrot&celery
&onion/bay/t pepcorn.
Simmr h.
Sieve.
Yld8c.

FISH STOCK

Bring to simmr lb bones
&head/5c h2o/c wtwine/
t wtpepcorn/BqtGrni; skim.
Simmr20m.
Strain w muslin.
Yld5c.

KEEP A 4-QUART CONTAINER
in the freezer for vegetable
scraps (no brassicas or
eggplant). When full, it's
time to make Vegetable
Scrap Stock.

TIP

Ⓜ VEGETABLE SCRAP STOCK

Sauté onion&carrot&
celery/2T garlc&oil.
+8c h2o&vegscraps/BqtGrni/
T salt/t pepcorn; boil.
Simmr30m.
Strain.
Yld6c.

Ⓥ BROWN VEGETABLE SCRAP STOCK

Brwn onion/2T oil alone before proceeding with the sauté step in Scrap Stock; +T soya&worces to finish.

TIP

THE NEXT THREE STOCKS MAKE simple soups: Ladle over hot al dente Fresh Noodles, then top with soy sauce, scallions, chilies, ham and egg.

CHINESE STOCK

Boil lb chicken&porkbone/ 5c h2o/2carrot&onion/scored thumb ging/t salt& wtpepcorn; skim.
Simmr3h.
Strain,cool.
Yld4c.

DASHI

JAPAN In pot, soak4"dry kombu&shiitake/4c h2o 20m.
Boil; +⅓c loose bonito.
Cool5m,strain,press.
Yld4c.

ZESTY STOCK

Boil dbl batch(8c)Chicken or Scrap Stock/3"scored ging/ 2 lemgrass&hotchili&limeleaf (opt); immr20m.
Strain.
Yld6c.

BREADS
& SAVORY PIES

Baking is a process, but need not be laborious. In fact, most breads require only short periods of sustained focus, and then some waiting. It's a meditative pleasure well-suited to a leisurely Sunday, and you get to start the week with a breadbox full of your own tender blueberry muffins, savory and salt-flecked Jewish pletzels or tangy sourdough for sandwiches.

All of this is made even easier with the right tools: a few large bowls, nonstick bakeware, and a dough scraper—a hard, thin piece of metal or plastic that makes gathering or dividing dough and cleaning up kneading surfaces a snap. If you have or prefer regular bakeware, it never hurts to lightly oil and flour it before adding dough or batter to ensure that the baked goods don't stick.

Quick breads and muffins are definitely the easiest to master, but making yeast-risen breads is less mysterious than you might think. Success really boils down to two essentials: kneading and temperature. Kneading must be done vigorously for at least seven minutes; the error of overkneading is nearly impossible to commit, except by machine. You'll know you've kneaded enough when the dough feels barely sticky and thoroughly smooth, warm and slightly elastic—bouncing back just a little when you press your fingertips against it.

As for yeast, it's a living organism, so treat it gently. Mix it with water that's body-temperature warm, and for the first rise, place dough in a large, clean bowl, then cover with plastic wrap and a tea towel to help coax the yeast into action. For the second rise, shape and place dough, again covered, either in loaf pans for pan loaves; in other pans for treats like cinnamon knots; or in floured, cloth-lined, large bowls for round loaves. (The latter are turned over onto a preheated baking sheet, so use a smooth, not fluffy, cloth to line the bowl so the dough doesn't stick to it.) And right before baking, slash tops with a razor blade and create your signature mark, whether that be a cross, diamond, spiral, or whatever you like.

For yeast breads, preheat the oven a little above temperature to ensure a golden brown crust. Adjust it back down as soon as the dough goes in. The bread is done once it smells great, makes a hollow noise when tapped and the top is well browned. Wait until it cools to slice it, if you can stand it.

QUICK BREADS

TO MEASURE DRY INGREDIENTS ACCURATELY, OVERSCOOP FROM
the source, then sweep the excess off the top with your fingers or
a knife.

BANANA BREAD

Cream3brbanana/
¼c buttr&sug&milk/½c brsug.
Fold+c flr/½c whtflr/t bkgpdr&
soda&cinn/¼t salt.
Fill grsdloafpan.
h@350°F.

CHEESE BREAD

Mix3c flr/T bkgpdr/
¼t cayenne&pep/c
dicedcheddar.
Fold+mixd 2c buttrmilk/
btnegg/3T oil.
Fill grsdloafpan; top w parm.
h@350°F.

UBIQUITOUS AT IRISH mealtimes, this lofty domed bread is easy to make but impressively artisanal in looks. Serve thickly sliced with butter.

SODA BREAD

IRELAND Cut¾c buttr/
3c flr&whtflr/2t salt&soda/
¼c brsug. Fold+2c buttrmilk.
Form rough dome on
flrdbkgsheet. h@375°F.
Set12h.

THIS HEAVY, DARK AND slightly sour Soda Rye makes nice toast, open-face sandwiches or hors d'oeuvres. Slice thinly to serve.

SODA RYE

Mix2½c ryeflr/t soda&cumIn &salt/½t bkgpdr/c yogurt/
½c milk/2T honey.
Spread in grsdloafpan.
45m@400°F; +30m@350°F.

COCOA-ZUCCHINI LOAF

Beat egg/½c sug&oil;
+c shreddedzuke/t vanil.
Mix+2c flr/9T brsug&cocoa/
2t bkgpdr/t soda.
Fill grsdloafpan. h@325°F.

PUMPKIN LOAF

Mix c flr/t bkgpdr&
SweetSpice/¼t salt. Fold+btn
c canpumpkin/egg/
⅓c brsug&oil.
Fill grsdloafpan. 50m@350°F.

APPLE MUFFINS

Mix c flr/⅓c brsug/
t bkgpdr&SweetSpice/¼t salt.
Fold+btn ⅓c milk/egg/
2T mltdbuttr; +½c grtdapple/
¼c walnut.
Fill6. 20m@350°F.

BACON MUFFINS

Sift c flr/1½t bkgpdr&sug/
¼t salt&cayenne.
Fold+mixd egg/½c milk/
2T mltdlard(or buttr)&fried
bacon. Fill6. 22m@375°F.

BANANA MUFFINS

Mix c flr/½pkg banana
pudding/t bkgpdr&cinn/
½t salt/¼c milk&oil&
sug&bran&walnt(opt)
/brbanana.
Fill6,top w cinn&sug.
25m350°F.

BLUEBERRY MUFFINS

Soak½c oats&buttrmilk/
btnegg/2T mltdbuttr.
Fold+mixd ½c flr/c berry/
¼c brsug/¼t bkgpdr/
½t soda&salt.
Fill6.
22m@375°F.

BRAN MUFFINS

Mix½c flr&whtbran/
3T brsug/t bkgpdr/¼t salt&
cinn. Fold+mixd 2T oil/
egg/½c milk&raisin(opt).
Fill6. 20m@400°F.

CRANBERRY MUFFINS

Mix c flr/¼c sug/
½t soda&cinn/¼t salt.
Fold+btn ½c applesauce/
egg/3T oil; +½c cranberry/
¼c nuts.
Fill6.
30m@350°F.

PUMPKIN MUFFINS

Soak c bran/½c candpumpkin/
egg/3T milk&oil.
Fold+mixd c flr/3T sug/
1½t bkgpdr/¼t soda&
SweetSpice.
Fill6.
25m@350F.

SKILLET BISCUITS

Mix1½c flr/t salt/T bkgpdr.
Cut+½c buttr; gatherup+
¾c milk.
Roll,cut12.
Brwn4m/side@med on
grsdskillet.

@RHODACOOK'S BISCUITS

Mix c flr/1½t bkgpdr/
¼t salt/⅛t soda.
Cut+2T buttr;
mix+⅓c srcrm, 2T milk.
Knead gently.
Roll,cut6.
12m@450F.

Ⓜ SCONES

Mix2c flr/½t salt/T bkgpdr/
3T sug.
Cut+6T buttr. Fold+c lgtcrm.
Form crumbly disk;
cut8wedges.
Top w sug.
Bake17m@400°F.

THIS IS FROM A CHARMING
artist I met on Twitter. I
developed the Scones tweet
at his request. In return,
he sweetened them up
for high tea.

TIP

Ⓥ @CLAYRIVERS' SCONES

Mix2c flr/½t salt/T bkgpdr/
3T sug.
Cut+5T buttr..
Fold +c crm/T orangezest&
clottedcrm/⅓c drycranberry.
Continue w Scones.

THESE ARE LIKE CREAM PUFF
shells, but cheesy. A little
crunchy outside, moist and
delicate within, they're best
eaten hot from the oven.

TIP

PAO DE QUEIJO

BRAZIL Scald c milk/t salt/
½c buttr.
Beat+2c maniocflr; knead+
c parm/2egg.
Roll20balls; top w parm.
Puff,brwn~15m@400°F.

YEAST BREADS

FOR A PAN LOAF, PAT RISEN DOUGH INTO AN OVAL SLAB. ROLL snugly from one short end, pinch seam, and put seam down in loaf pan for 2nd rise.

FOR A ROUND LOAF, PUT RISEN DOUGH IN A LARGE FLOURED, cloth-lined bowl for 2nd rise. To bake, turn dough over onto preheated pan.

FOR LOAVES THAT STAY FRESH AND TENDER LONGER, SAVE unsalted water when you next boil potatoes and use that as the water when making dough.

THE BEST HOME BAKER I know, Rhoda Cook, taught me this recipe, which I use often. It makes 2 plain pan or round loaves and many variations.

EACH OF THESE VARIATIONS uses a half batch of @rhodacook's Bread dough, so you can make two different types—maybe one sweet and one savory.

Ⓜ @RHODACOOK'S BREAD

Warm3T sug&oil/T salt/
2c h2o; +mixd c flr/
2T yeast&whtgerm. Knead
+4c flr. Cvr,rise h; +40m as
2loaf.
30m@375°F.

Ⓥ BROWN BREAD

+T molasses mixd w the h2o;
increase whtgerm to ¼c.
When kneading, sub½ the flr
w wht or other whlgrain flr.
Yld2loaf.

Ⓥ COCONUT SPIRALS

When forming one pan loaf,
top½dough slab rolled
9"x12" w 4T mltdbuttr&sug/
c tstdcocont/t SweetSpice.

Ⓥ HERB BREAD

Mince¼c mild(eg basil/dill)
or I strong(eg rosemry/sage)
fresh herbs.
When forming one pan loaf,
sprinkle on ½dough slab.

Ⓥ OLIVE BREAD

Use extra-virgin olvoil for oil.
When forming one pan loaf,
sprinkle½c chopdolive on
½dough slab.

Ⓥ ONION BREAD

Sauté partly cvrd 2c onion/
T olvoil@med-low~40m to
caramelize.
When forming one pan loaf,
sprinkle on ½dough slab.

Ⓥ RAISIN BREAD

Soak½c raisin/c hot blktea~h.
Drain,pat dry.
When forming one pan loaf,
sprinkle on ½dough slab+
T mltdbuttr&sug/2t cinn(opt).

TIP

THESE VARIATIONS ARE NOT
in loaf form. For the Cinnamon
Knots, tie rolled lengths of
dough by crossing both ends
and looping one through.

Ⓥ CINNAMON KNOTS

Cut½batch risen dough
in 9pce. Roll 6"e.
Dip in c mltdbuttr; mixd
c sug/3T cinn. Knot,tuck
in sqpan for 2nd rise.
20m@375°F.

TIP

TRY APPLES, PLUMS, PEACHES
or apricots on this homey
treat.

Ⓥ FRUIT FOCCACIA

Roll½batch risendough on
grsd&flrd deepbkgsheet.
Top w ¼c sug&softbuttr/
5c fruit/¼c lem&sug; rise 20m.
Prick.
20m@450°F.

Ⓥ HERB FOCACCIA

Roll½batch risendough on
lrg grsd&flrd bkgsheet.
Top w ⅓c olvoil&olv(opt)/
T coarsesalt&rosemry; rise
20m. Prick.
12m@500°F.

Ⓥ ROLLS

Cut½batch risendough in
9pce. With oiled hands form
balls,group in sqpan for 2nd
rise. 20m@375°F.
Brush w T mltdbuttr while hot.

ALMOND BREAD

Boil,cool½c grndalmond/
c milk; +t yeast; +2c flr/
2T sug/egg/t salt.
Knead~½c flr,rise h; +45m
as pan or round loaf.
25m@375°F.

SOURDOUGH STARTER IS EASY to make with rye flour: it ferments steadily for artisanal flavor and crumb. A 32-oz jar is ideal for storage.

TIP

NEW SOURDOUGH STARTER

Mix⅛t yeast/½c h2o&flr;
cvr w cloth~36h.
Mix+c h2o/2c ryeflr;
cvr w cloth~24h.
Chill12-24h.
Keeps up to 7d.

SOURDOUGH BREAD

Top Starter w 2c rye&wht flr
8h. Mix+3c h2o/t salt.
Rsv½,knead+c h2o/T salt/
4c flr,rise3h Form 2roundloaf.
10m@500°F;+h@425°F.

PUT RESERVED HALF OF Starter in fridge. If not used in 1 week, it must be renewed. Split to make two Renewed Starters or discard half.

TIP

RENEWED SOURDOUGH STARTER

Mix e ½ rsvd Starter +c h2o/
2c ryeflr; refrigerate1-2d.
Before use, cvr w cloth~
24h@roomtemp.
Keeps 7d.

LIKE ALL FLATBREADS, KESRA is versatile. It's dipped in every dish in Morocco, from Bissara to Honey Tagine, and easily fits other cuisines.

TIP

KESRA

MOROCCO Mix T yeast/
t sug/¼c h2o,knead+
4c flr/⅓c cornmeal/2t salt/
2T mltdbuttr/1½ c h2o.
Rise2 8"disc h,prick.
5m@450°F; +15m@375°F.

NO WONDER THE ORIGINAL recipe for this, by NY baker Jim Lahey, caught fire online: a crusty loaf with an airy, chewy inside and no kneading!

NO-KNEAD BREAD
Mix4c flr/2t salt/½t yeast/
2c h2o.
Rise18h@70°; +2h as
round loaf.
Flr,flip to preheateddutchoven.
Cvr30m@450°; +20m
uncvrd.

THIS IMITATES A DARK Northern Irish loaf whose company recipe is top secret. It's best when toasted. Dark corn syrup may replace malt syrup.

VEDA
Mix T yeast/5T h2o; +mixd
2T mltdbuttr&maltsyrup&
molasses&brsug/t salt.
Knead+c flr&wht flr.
Rise h; +20m as pan loaf.
30m@400°F.

SAVORY PIES

BASIC PIZZA DOUGH

ITALY Mix2t yeast/t salt/
c flr&warm h2o.
Knead+1½c flr; cvr,rise h.
Roll to fit 14"x16" bkgsheet
or 2 12"pizzapans.

Ⓜ PIZZA MARINARA

Drape BasicPizzaDough on
cornmeal-dusted 14"x16"
bkgsheet or 2 12"pizzapans;
+3T olvoil/1½c TomSauce.
20m@400°F.

SCATTER PIZZA MARINARA WITH
different toppings to create the
following variations.

TIP

Ⓥ PIZZA BIANCA

Omit TomSauce; +mixd 3T
pesto&olvoil/8oz ricotta/
garlc&s+p.

Ⓥ PIZZA CAPRICCIOSA

+6oz slicedmozz/½c fresh
tom&shroom&artichokeheart&
olv&pepperoni; carefully crack
egg on top(opt).

Ⓥ HAWAIIAN CLASSIC
+8oz grtdmozz/
c pineapple&cookdham/
½c onion&parm.

Ⓥ PIZZA MARGHERITA
+2c freshtom/½c basil&
parm/8oz slicedmozz/s+p.

Ⓥ NEW YORK CLASSIC
+8oz grtdmozz/c sliced
pepperoni/½c parm/
rdpep&garlc.

Ⓥ PIZZA QUATTRO
FORMAGGI
+4oz ricotta&sliced mozz&
fontina&gorgonzola(mixed or
separated in each of the four
quarters)/pep.

Ⓥ PIZZA ROMANA
+8oz slicedmozz/c freshtom/
2T mincdanchovy&oreg/pep.

Ⓥ PIZZA VIENNESE
+c freshtom/c slicedcookd
sausage/2T oreg&pep.

DEEP-DISH PIZZA
DOUGH
Mix T yeast/c h2o; +c flr/
¼c finecornmeal/2T oil.
Knead+2c flr,rise~h.
Roll,drape in 10"springform
pan or ironskillet.

TRY THESE DEEP-DISH PIZZA
toppings: bellpep/broccoli/
spinach/shroom/cookdmeat/
artichokeheart/olv/pineapple/
feta/onion/basil/jalapeño.

TIP

DEEP-DISH PIZZA
Oil draped
DeepDishPizzaDough.
Bakeblind5m@400°F.
Lyr w 16oz mozz/2c any
toppings/½c parm/
3c TomSauce.
40m@400°F.

CUTTING FLOUR AND FAT together achieves oil-bonded flour that toasts up (flavor) and bits of fat that melt, leaving pockets of air (texture).

TO MEASURE BUTTER, ADD TO water in a large measuring cup until the water rises by the required amount. A ½ cup is 8 tablespoons, or 1 stick.

CREAM PASTRY DOUGH

Per dbl 9"pie crust,
cut½c buttr/2c flr.
Sprinkle+½c crm;
gather,form ball.
Wrap,chill30m.

SAVORY STRUDEL DOUGH

Cut2T buttr/c flr&mashdtater.
Knead+2t yeast/2T warm
h2o. Rise h.
On flrdcloth gently
roll,pull20"sq.
Trim,buttr.

LEEK PIE

Sauté5c leek/
2T buttr&bacon&h2o/
⅛t nutmeg&s+p.
Fill CreamPastryDough,
cut vent.
40m@400°F.
Pour mixd 3T milk/egg in vent;
bake15m+.

TO MAKE THIS UNUSUAL sweet and savory filled pastry, choose a milder blue cheese, such as Danish or Cashel.

BLUE APPLE STRUDEL

Top StrudelDough w brdcrumb.
Mix2c apple/½c bluecheese/
s+p.
Put on doughedge.
Roll,buttr,30m@350°F
(buttr1x).

MUSHROOM STRUDEL

Top StrudelDough w
brdcrumb.
Sauté6c shroom/c shallot/
2T buttr&dill&wine.
Put on doughedge.
Roll,buttr,30m@350F
(buttr1x).

TIP

PUFF PASTRY MAY BE LIGHTLY
rolled for crusts or pulled to
22"x22" (a floured tablecloth
helps) and used for hors
d'oeuvres.

PUFF PASTRY DOUGH

Toss½c dicedbuttr/1½c flr/
½t salt; +t lem/iced h2o.
Roll,fold in thirds;
rpt roll&fold2x.
Wrap,chill30m.
Yld lb.

SUMMER QUICHE

In pieplate lyr PuffPastry
Dough/slicedtom/s+p/
T basil/½slicedeggplant/
½c feta.
Rpt veg; +mixd 4egg/
c crm/s+p.
45m@400°F.

TIP

EASILY CONFUSED DUE TO
similar names, Betzels are a
fried pastry filled with egg,
herbs and feta, and Pletzels
are crusty baked flatbreads.

BETZELS

ALGERIA Mix1raw/6boiled egg/
c feta/⅓c garlc&mint&parsly&
olv/T paprka.
Cut PuffPastry in 4strip,
triangle-fold w T mix e.
Deepfry~6m.

PLETZEL

JEWISH Mix t yeast/c h2o&flr; knead+t salt/2T olvoil/c flr. Rise2h.
Top4discs w t oil&poppyseed/ ¼t coarsesalt/T onion e. 12m@475°F.

LAHMACUN

TURKEY Knead T yeast/t sug& salt/1½c h2o/2c flour; rise h.
Quarter,roll,oil; top w mixed 2c feta&cookedspinach.
15m@450°F.
Srv w lem.

BREAKFAST

Why not reclaim the morning as a time for little feasts? They need not be elaborate—even a handful of toasty homemade granola scattered over thick yogurt or a bowl of seasonal fruit salad to go with your coffee is a victory against the breakfast blahs.

Take advantage of the weekend by pulling out all the stops. Invite your favorite conversationalists for brunch and heap their plates with sweet and savory comfort foods from around the world: Brittany's lacy buckwheat galettes, kissed with homemade jam; buttery Irish potato pancakes called farls, hot off the skillet; sizzling Mexican tortilla and egg migas, topped with fresh salsa verde and cilantro; or a tall stack of winsome American pancakes. Once the plates are empty, just keep the coffee cups full for fantastic social effect.

EGGS

TIP

TEST THE FRESHNESS OF EGGS IN a big bowl of water. Fresh eggs will sink or bob; if an egg fully floats, it is old and should be discarded.

BAKED EGGS

Fill4muffincups w pinch s+p&thyme&dill/t buttr e. Mlt@300°F; +T cookdveg or meat(opt)/egg/T parm&crm e. 15m@300°F.

BASIC BOILED EGGS

Bring to full boil 1-6egg/h2o to cvr; simmr3m for creamy, med-set yolk(-/+m for soft/ firm).
Rmv from h2o.

FRIED EGGS

Heat hvypan 5m@low; +T buttr,heat until foam subsides.
Quickly+1-4egg/s+p.
Cvr3m for soft yolk(-/+30s for runny/firm).

THE VOLUME OF WATER IN the recipe below keeps the temperature very stable and yields boiled eggs with tender whites and silky soft yolks.

USE FRESH HERBS, QUALITY eggs and semi-firm grated cheeses such as cheddar, Swiss or Monterey Jack, unless otherwise specified.

PERFECT SOFT-BOILED EGGS

Heat12c h2o to simmr; +3-8egg. Maintain at near simmring(not bubbling) uncvrd6m. Rmv from h2o.

Ⓜ FRENCH-STYLE OMELET

Per srvg, beat2egg/s ı p. Mlt2t buttr@med-high past foaming; +eggs. Lift,tilt to let run under until halfset. Fill,fold.

Ⓜ AMERICAN-STYLE OMELET

For 2srvg, whip3T crm; fold+5btnegg/s+p. Mlt2T buttr@med; +eggs. When ½set+½c cheese; finish6m@400°F. Fill,fold.

Ⓥ ASPARAGUS PARMESAN OMELET

Per srvg, trim, blanch5aspargus. Beat½lemzest w egg. Fill omelet w ¼c parm (or chevre)/aspargus.

ⓥ CHEDDAR MARMALADE OMELET

Per srvg, mix T any marmalade/~dash oj.
Fill omelet w ¼c cheddar/marmalade mix.
Top w zest.

TIP

THESE CAN BE MADE WITH either thin French or fluffy American omelets. For the latter, remember to double fillings and use an oven-safe pan.

ⓥ APPLE PECAN OMELET

Per srvg, sauté pce bacon; +t buttr/⅓c apple/dash cinn.
Mix+T maple.
Fill omelet w ¼c cheddar/apple mix/2T tstdpecan.

ⓥ SIMPLE CHEESE OMELET

Per srvg, fill omelet w ½c emmental(or other cheese)/mixd ¼t dijon/T CrèmeFraîche or srcrm.

ⓥ CRANBERRY BRIE OMELET

Per srvg, brwn,dice pce bacon(opt). Fill omelet w 2oz slicedbrie/3T Cranberry Sauce/bacon/T parsly.

ⓥ DENVER OMELET

Per srvg, sauté 2T onion&bellpep&buttr; +¼c cookdham/s+p 2m.
Fill omelet w ¼c cheddar/ham mix.
Garnish w parsly.

ⓥ GREEK OMELET

Per srvg, beat T oreg w eggs.
Fill omelet w 2T olv&feta&tom&bellpep.
Garnish w oreg/lemslices.

ⓥ HERB OMELET

Per srvg, beat2T mild(basil/cilantro/dill) or T med-strong (chive/thyme) or ½t strong rosemry/tarrgn)herb w eggs.
Garnish w herb.

Ⓥ HUNGARIAN OMELET

Per srvg, brwn,chop
⅓c sausage; sauté+
2T onion/t oil.
Fill omelet w ¼c gouda/
3T Lecsó/sausage mix.
Garnish w parsly.

Ⓥ MARGHERITA OMELET

Per srvg, beat mincdgarlc
w eggs. Fill omelet w
¼c shreddedmozz/diced
roma/T basil/dash rdpep.
Garnish w basil/parm.

Ⓥ MUSHROOM CHEESE OMELET

Per srvg, heat T buttr
@med-high past foaming;
+c shroom/T parsly/
dash nutmeg.
Fill omelet w ⅓c emmental/
shroom mix.

Ⓥ PEPPERS AND CHICKEN OMELET

Per srvg, sauté2T onion/
T buttr; +⅓c cookdchicken
&bellpep/dash blk&wt pep.
Fill omelet w ¼c jack/chicken
mlx.

Ⓥ SMOKED SALMON OMELET

Per srvg, beat½lemzest/
T dill w eggs.
Fill omelet w ¼c edam/
T mayo&mincdlem w rind/
¼c smokedsalmon.
Top w lemslices.

Ⓥ WALDORF OMELET

Per srvg, mix
2T apple&grape&tstdwalnt;/
T mayo(or yogurt)/
t lem&chive/s+p.
Fill omelet w ¼c gouda/
apple mix.

Ⓜ POACHED EGGS

In skillet, simmr2"h2o/
t salt/2T vinegr;
+1-4egg one at a time.
Cvr offheat 4m for med(-/+m
for soft/firm); spoon out.

Ⓥ SCRAMBLED EGGS

Beat8egg/½t s+p/
½c milk to just bubbly.
Mlt T buttr@high.
Slowly stir/fold egg across
pan~2m until set but still wet.

TIP

MY GOOD FRIEND @IRONIX
is passionate about particle
physics and scrambled eggs.
This version of which is
especially tasty.

@IRONIX'S SCRAMBLED EGGS

For a richer brunch dish,
+extra egg; use⅓c cream&
parm in place of milk.

BRUNCH DISHES

CORN CAKES

Beat egg/½c milk;
+ c cornmeal/T flr&mltdbuttr/
½t salt/t bkgpdr.
Ladle in grsdpan@med;
flip when bubbling.

HASH BROWNS

Peel,grt2lb lrg waxytater; toss
+2T olvoil/T mltdbuttr/s+p.
Scatter on bkgsheet.
20m@400°F; turn occas
(+T oil if dry)~25m.

HOME FRIES

Chop2lb tater.
Fry+¼c oil 10m@med; turn.
Fry,turn occas(+T oil if dry) to
gold. Fry@high to brwn; s+p.
Srv w srcrm&salsa.

"FARLS" MEANS "QUARTERS," referring to how these mashed-potato flatbreads are cut into four. Serve at breakfast or tea, toasted and buttered.

Ⓜ FARLS

IRELAND Fold2c well-mashdtater/¼c flr/
T milk&mltdbuttr/⅛t salt.
On flrdsurface form¼"disc.
Quarter,brwn in dryskillet.
Srv hot.

Ⓥ CHEESE FARLS

+¼c grtd agedcheddar (or other med-strong cheese) to mashdtaters in Farls.

SPREAD EITHER BATTER IN the pan with a swiftly tilting motion. If it seems to be setting too quickly, add a teaspoon of water to the batter.

CRÊPES

FRANCE Beat c h2o&milk/
4egg/½t salt/
2c flr/¼c mltdbuttr.
Chill>2h.
In buttrd HOT pan@med
tilt¼c. Brwn; flip briefly.

IN BRITTANY, BUCKWHEAT galettes are filled with items such as ham and cheese. Fill sweet crêpes with sliced fruit, jam or Nutella.

GALETTES

FRANCE Beat 1½c buckwhtflr/
½t salt/c milk/2egg.
Beat+½c h2o/2T beer.
Chill>2h.
In buttrd HOT pan@med
tilt¼c.
Brwn; flip briefly.

FRENCH TOAST MAY BE MADE with sliced white bread, fresh or stale; cousin Pain Perdu ("lost bread") is best with stale baguette or brioche.

Ⓜ FRENCH TOAST

Whisk2egg/¼c buttr/
1½c milk/t vanil; +¼c sug/
⅔c flr/¼t salt.
Soak8pce bread~m.
Fry+T buttr~m/side
@med-high.

Ⓥ PAIN PERDU

Increase milk to 2c and reduce
flr to T in FrenchToast.

Ⓜ BAKED FRENCH TOAST

Beat4egg/¾c milk&crm/
t vanil&cinn.
Top6c cubedbread in
buttrdbkgdish.
Chill8h; top w
¼c mltdbuttr/⅓c brsug.
40m@350°F.

Ⓥ FRUIT-BAKED
FRENCH TOAST

Toss bread w c sm pces
fruit(eg orange, berry,
pineapple, banana, or
driedfruit)+extra to srv.

AMERICAN PANCAKES

Mix c flr/T sug/
t bkgpdr/¼t soda&salt;
+btn c milk/2T mltdbuttr/egg.
Mix lumpy.
Ladle on grsdpan@med; flip
when bubbling.

BUTTERMILK
PANCAKES

Mix c buttrmilk/egg/
2T mltdbuttr; +c flr/T sug/
½t bkgpdr&salt/¼t soda.
Ladle in grsdpan@med; flip
when bubbling.

OATMEAL PANCAKES

Soak c oats/1½c buttrmilk
overnight; +¼c flr/egg/
t bkgpdr&oil/dash salt.
Ladle in grsdpan@med; flip
when bubbling.

TIP

THIS FAMILY-SIZED PANCAKE is a convenient way to serve flapjacks without standing at the stove for a long time. Serve in wedges.

PANNUKAKKU

FINLAND Beat c flr/4egg/
2½c milk/¼c honey/
t salt. Heat ironskillet,
+¼c buttr,batter.
25m@425°F.
Srv w CherrySauce or maple.

RICE WAFFLES

Mix½c flr&rice krispies/
⅓c strch/½t bkgpdr/¼t soda&
salt; +yolk/½c milk/¼c oil/
2T honey.
Fold+softbtneggwt.
Bake on waffleiron.

LEMON WAFFLES

Mix c flr/t soda&salt/⅓c
sug/2T grndalmond; +egg/
T oil/¾c milk/t vanil.
Bake on waffleiron.
Top w reduced ⅓c lem/
T sug&buttr.

EGGS BENEDICT

Per srvg, lyr½tstd
englishmuffin/slice cookdham/
PoachedEgg on warm plate;
top w Hollandaise.

TIP

A FLEXIBLE AND FANTASTIC family-sized omelet, Frittata may also be filled with chopped and cooked potato, asparagus, onion, bacon, etc.

FRITTATA

Spread ironskillet@med w
T oil/shallot/c slicedtom&zuke/
s+p; +6btnegg.
Cvr,don't stir~9m@low;
20m@350°F.
Invert to srv+parm&basil.

MIGAS

MEXICO Chop,deepfry3corn tortilla. Sauté jalapeño&onion /2T oil. Stir+6btnegg to set; +c tom&scalion.
Srv w SalsaVerde&cilantro.

PIPERADA

SPAIN Saute garlc&onion/ T olvoil; +rd RoastedPepper/ ½c tom&smokedham 15m. Stir+4btnegg/s+p until set.

SOUFFLÉ

Mix4eggs/c grtdgouda/ ⅓c parm&srcrm/½t onlonsalt& grndmustard@med 30s; +@high10s.
Fill buttrd/parmdusted qt dish. Puff/brwn25m@350°F.

BREAD STRATA

Brwn c onion&veg/t paprka/ T buttr; +3c stalebread; +mixd c milk/3egg/ 2T basil&parsly.
Top w mixd ¼c crm& grtdcheese/s + p.
h@375°F.

TOFU SCRAM

Fry3T scalion&oil/t cumin& garlc; +2c mixdveg/t Curry Powder/lb mashdfirmtofu/ 3T soya&sherry/T hotsauce& sesoil&basil/s&p.

FRUITS & CEREALS

TIP

TO EASILY CUBE A MANGO, slice off each cheek from the fruit, score flesh in desired-size cubes, then flip skin inside-out and cut off cubes.

SPRING FRUIT SALAD

Toss3c rhubarb/sug.
15m@325°F in sm cvrddish.
Fold w juices/2c mango&
cherry&strawberry/
~2T HoneySyrup. Chill.
Yld~8c.

SUMMER FRUIT SALAD

Toss2c blueberry&strawberry&
honeydew&nectarine&water
melon/peach/2T BerrySyrup/
¼c lime/T rosewater&mint.
Chill.
Yld~10c.

AUTUMN FRUIT SALAD

Toss c gr&rd&concord grape/
¾pomegranate/2kiwi&pear&
persimmon/1-3T VanillaSyrup
&lem.
Chill; top w ¼pomegranate.
Yld~8c.

WINTER FRUIT SALAD

Mix gr&rdapple&asianpear/
T lem; toss w 2mandarin
&tangerine/c date&
kumquat/~3T GingerSyrup.
Chill; dust w cinn.
Yld~8c.

GRAPEFRUIT BRÛLÉE

Drizzle ¼t vanil or
flowerwater onto halvdfruit;
top w finelygrnd 2T sug/
¼t cardamom(opt).
Spoon onto halvdfruit.
Broil to brwn.

HOT PAPAYA SMOOTHIE

Puree2c papaya(or mango)/
c oj/½c yogurt/
3T honey&mint&lime/
t ging&jalapeño/dash salt.

@MAREN'S SUMMER YOGURT

Foodproc2c(pref greek)
yogurt/8freshfig/2wtpeach/
banana.
Top w tstdnuts&honey.

GRANOLA

Mix¼c molasses&oil/
½c applejuice/t vanil;
+4c quickoats/2c nuts/
½c flaxseed/2t cinn&ging/
½t nutmeg.
h@300°F on
2bkgsheet(stir3x).

OATMEAL NEEDN'T BE BLAND.
Try topping with one or more
of these: homemade jam,
chopped fruit, toasted nuts,
brown sugar, cinnamon,
yogurt.

TIP

BASIC OATMEAL

Boil2c h2o(or sub½milk);
+c oats/2T brsug(opt)/
⅛t salt&buttr(opt).
Simmr½cvrd~10m.

APPLE PIE PORRIDGE

Mix,simmr½c oats/1½c h2o/
dicedapple/½t cinn&vanil/
¼t buttr/dash salt in
ricecooker (or cvr15m@low).
Srv w maple.

SOUPS
& SALADS

Look to these recipes for stand-alone light lunches or the first course of a meal. I have absolutely no patience for anemic dishes, so each offers intrigue, flavor and satisfaction.

Soups and salads are also ideal dishes for spotlighting the best produce of the moment and become the sort of memorable seasonal specialties you'll both anticipate and return to: a celadon-hued pea and radish greens soup that sings of spring; a melon and blackberry soup, aromatic with rosewater and mint, to cool your summer days; a broiled salad of romaine and grapes that's lovely when the first chilly nights of autumn hit; and @kellan's fennel and pomegranate salad, crisp and tart and colorful, to brighten up your winter.

A few tools will help in their preparation. An immersion blender allows you to puree soups without the nuisance of transferring them to a blender (see the Tools section for more information about immersion blenders). A big salad spinner gets your greens from mud-speckled to sparkling in short order. Finally, invest in a set of attractive bowls that may be heated or chilled so you can present your soups and salads with panache.

COLD SOUPS

THE CREAMY HASS AVOCADO works best for soup. They should be just on the firm side of ripe; save the really ripe ones for Guacamole.

COLD AVOCADO SOUP

Puree 1½avocado/½shallot/peeldcuke/3c buttrmilk/s+p; chill.
Top w pulse-blended ½avocado&shallot/tom/2T lime&yogurt&basil.

CHERRY SOUP

HUNGARY Simmr20m
lb srcherry/3c rosé/¼t cinn.
Puree+t flr/2T Crème Fraîche&lem; simmr thick. Chill.
Srv w CrèmeFraîche.

TIP

CHIPOTLES ARE SMOKED jalapeño peppers, available canned in adobo sauce or dried (soak in hot water to use in place of canned).

GAZPACHO

SPAIN Mince,mix tom& bellpep&cuke&shallot& garlc&chipotle; +2c tomjuice/ 2T cilantro&sherry/lime&zest. Chill.
Top w olvoil/s+p.

MELON GAZPACHO

Mix,chill2c pureedmelon/ ¾c cuke&tom&oj/ ½c rdonion/3T ricevinegr& cilantro&chive&oil/2t worces/ cayenne&s+p to taste.

MELON & BLACKBERRY SOUP

Puree,chill½sm watermelon &honeydew/lem&lime;
+c sparklingwine/T rosewater.
Top w melonballs/c blackberry/ mint.

TIP

THIS RADISH SOUP IS ALSO wonderful served hot.

RADISH SOUP

Sauté2c radish/⅓c buttr.
Mix+¼c flr; +c wtwine&crm/ 3c milk.
Puree.
Simmr15m+bay/salt&wtpep.
Srv w dill.

HOT SOUPS

TIP

THIS IS A BEAUTIFUL PALATE cleanser; my elegant friend @miju serves it in demitasses, topped with toasted sliced almonds and cream liqueur.

ALMOND SOUP

Simmr c grndalmond/3c Stock/ whlonion/clove&bay 30m. Sieve; +½c milk/ ⅛t nutmeg&s+p. Brwn2T buttr&flr; +soup. Simmr5m; +c crm.

ASPARAGUS SOUP

DENMARK Trim lb aspargus. Cut,blanch tips; steam stalks 5m. Brwn T buttr&flr; simmr+stalks/2c Stock 5m. Puree+c crm; +tips.

AUTUMN SOUP

Mix¼c oil/dicebuttrnutsquash &tater&leek/t garlc&s+p& thyme&paprka; h@350°F. Puree+3c hot h2o. Srv w T tstdpumpkinseed &sunflrseed.

TIP AVGOLEMONO, AN EPHEMERAL dish that translates humbly to "egg broth," is used as both soup and sauce (see Sauces). Use Chicken Stock.

SOUPA AVGOLEMONO

GREECE Boil4c Stock;
+⅓c arborio or pastini
to tender.
Whip2eggwt; whisk+2yolk/
½c lem&pastaliquid.
Mix w soup/salt&wtpep.

TIP THIS RECIPE IS FROM A friend who's writing a novel about her family's history in Russia, the origin of this rustic, nourishing soup.

IRENE'S BORSCHT

Brwn onion&garlc/2T buttr;
+c beet&tom&h2o,simmr40m,
+c tater&carrot&cabbage/
3c Stock 20m;
+3T rdvinegr&dill.
Top w srcrm.

HOT AVOCADO SOUP

Puree2avocado/4c Stock/
T lem/salt+wtpep/nutmeg;
+c crm. Heat gently.
Top w crm/tstdcumin.

TIP I FIRST TASTED THIS AT A souk in Fez. Ladled piping hot, lavished with olive oil and cumin and served with Kesra bread, it's irresistible.

BISSARA

MOROCCO Brwn2T garlc/
¼c oil; +c soakedfava/
4c h2o/c parsly/t cumin&
paprka&salt&rdpep.
Simmr h,puree.
Top w olvoil&lem&cumin.

CREAM OF CARROT SOUP

Boil3c carrot/h2o to cvr/
2T rdlentll/t salt&garlc
until soft.
Puree+2c hotmilk&Stock.
Simmr10m; top w
nutmeg&pep.

MISO CARROT SOUP

Simmr~10m 4c Dashi/
c carrot&celery.
Puree or mix +2T brmiso.
Warm; +lem&wasabi
&scalion to taste.

TIP

IF YOU'RE IN THE MOOD FOR
a dish that excels at subtlety,
try this fragrant and mild
soup. The cauliflower may be
replaced with more potato.

CAULIFLOWER SOUP

Sauté onion/T olvoil; +t garlc
&caraway/med chopd cauliflr/
2c peeld tater/2c Stock/
BqtGrni.
Simmr@low~5m;
+¼c crm/s+p.

CREAM OF CELERY SOUP

Brwn2c onion/4c celery w
leaves/2T buttr; +t garlc 2m;
+4c Stock/¼c wtwine/BqtGrni.
Simmr10m; puree +c crm/
s+p.

THE EGGS IN THIS SOUP
are not fully cooked. As such,
don't serve to the elderly,
immuno-compromised,
or small children.

TIP

CELERIAC VELOUTÉ

Brwn T buttr&flr;
mix+4c stock.
Peel,steam2c celeriac; simmr
+3T buttr 15m; +stock 20m.
Puree+3btn yolk/¼c crm&
mltdbuttr.

VELOUTÉS ARE LITERALLY
"velvet" soups, incredibly rich
and served in small portions.
They may also be used as
sauces for meat or pasta.

TIP

BLACK PEPPER CHOWDER

Sauté2T buttr&basil/onion/
t salt; +2c rootveg&corn
&shroom/T pep&garlc 5m.
Simmr+3c h2o; ½puree.
Heat+3c milk.

FENNEL, BEAN & LIME SOUP

Sauté onion&fennel/2T oil;
+2c tom&cookdwtbean&h2o/
t garlc&oreg&limezest/s+p.
Boil; +½c pastina 10m.
Srv w lime.

CURRIED SOUP

Brwn onion&garlc/T sesoil
&olvoil; simmer+c zuke&yam/
3c h2o/2t CurryPowder&sug/
¼t cayenne&s+p 20m.
Puree+can cocont/¼c lime.

DARJEELING SOUP

Sauté leek&onion/T buttr.
Simmr15m+2c cauliflr/tater&
celery/4c Darjeeling tea/
s+p/bay.
Rmv bay; puree+⅓c crm.
Top w nutmeg&pep.

TO SAVE AN OVERSALTED
soup, stew, or sauce, simmer
with a few peeled and coarsely
chopped floury potatoes.
Remove before serving.

TIP

CORN SOUP

Kernel4c corn
Boil cobs/5c h2o/t salt; strain.
Sauté garlic&onion&celery/
s+p/2T oil.
Simmr9m; puree+cobstock
&3c corn.
Heat+c corn&crm.

GARDEN SOUP

Brwn,chop2chorizo;
+½c onion&carrot&grbean&
bellpep.
Simmr+3c tom&Stock/
¼c orzo 9m; +bnch chard/
¼c basil&parsly&wine/s+p.

GARDEN CHICKEN SOUP

Brwn onion/½lb chopdchicken/
3T oil; +t s+p/2T wtwine/
BqtGrni/2c bellpep&carrot&
tom/c orzo/4c h2o.
Simmr15m.
Top w parm.

MARIA'S GRAPEFRUIT SOUP

MEXICO Cvr,simmr2peeled grapefruit/h2o to cvr/dash cinn&salt&cayenne.
When fruit falls apart mix+ 2T honey.
Srv hot.

TIP **FIRM FRENCH LENTILLES DU PUY** have the best texture for this soup, but brown lentils may also be used. Serve it chunky or blended to taste.

LEMON LENTIL SOUP

Dice,sauté onion&celery& carrot&garlc/3T oil.
Cvr7m@low; +4c Stock/ c lentildupuy/BqtGrni& lemzest.
Simmr40m.
Puree+lem/s+p.

TIP **MEANING "WAKAME SOUP," THIS** birthday dish is said to bring good fortune in the coming year and is also eaten for health during pregnancy.

MIYEOK GUK

KOREA Soak,chop oz dried wakame.
Sauté+T sesoil/t garlc&ging; +3c Stock/2T soya.
Simmr30m.
Srv hot or cool; w chive& sesoil&pep.

MINESTRA DI VERDURE

ITALY Brwn¼c olvoil/c onion &celery&carrot&leek/garlc.
Boil+2c h2o&tom&zuke/ BqtGrni/s+p; +⅓c pastini 9m.

MUSHROOM SOUP

Sauté, cvr3T buttr/lb shroom &leek/½t thyme 5m@med.
Uncvr; +4c Stock.
Cvr,simmr20m.
Blend+½c crm/s+p.
Top w ⅓c sautéedshroom.

TIP

IF YOU FIND NETTLES THAT
are young and tender, use the
whole plant. Otherwise, use
only the topmost leaves. Wear
gloves if picking wild.

TIP

MOST TENDER SPRING RADISH
greens can be eaten; look for
fuzzy as opposed to prickly
leaves. They have a fresh,
delicately spicy flavor.

NETTLE SOUP

Sauté2T buttr/2shallot&garlc;
+4c Stock&nettles.
Cvr,simmr10m; puree+
¼c yogurt/nutmeg&
s+p to taste.

ONION SOUP

Sauté~h@low
¼c buttr/4onion/t salt;
+8c Stock/½c wine/
T worces/BqtGrni 20m.
Top e bowl w pce baguette/
3T gruyere&asiago; broil.

PAPPA AL POMODORO

ITALY Roast lb tom/T olvoil
20m@350°F.
Sauté T garlc&olvoil;
+3c tom&h2o/½c basil.
Simmr15m; +roast tom/
c cubedbread/s + p.

RADISH GREENS SOUP

Sauté onion/2T buttr;
cvr3m+4c young
radishgreens.
Simmr10m+c pea/2c Stock;
+⅓c mint/3c Stock/s+p 5m.
Sieve,heat + ⅓c crm.

MINTED PEA SOUP

Sauté tater&onion/T buttr&
garlc; +3T wtwine.
Simmr15m+4c Stock/
3T rice/2c peas/sprg parsly;
+mincdgarlc/3T mint/s+p.

SPLIT PEA SOUP

Drwn2c onion&carrot/
2T oil; +t garlc&paprka&
rosemry&thyme/bay/
8c Stock/2c peas/
hambone(opt)/s+p.
Simmr h,

BAKED POTATO SOUP

Sauté leek/T buttr;
+¼t cayenne&celeryseed&
paprka/bellpep/2c bakedtater;
+4c Stock; simmr10m.
Puree+2c milk/T dill/s+p.

GARLIC POTATO SOUP

Foil-wrap3sm tater/peeld
onion/whlgarlc h@375°F.
Cool,squeeze garlc from skin.
Simmr5m all+4c Stock.
Puree+⅓c srcrm/s+p.

TIP

IN IRELAND, FRESH DULSE,
a red seaweed, is added to
flavor sandwiches and soup.
Try other fresh or soaked dried
seaweeds (eg wakame), too.

DULSE & POTATO SOUP

IRELAND Cube 2waxytaters;
boil+¼c dulse/bay/h2o to cvr.
Simmr20m; +t buttr/
lem&s+p to taste.
Srv w SodaBread.

PUMPKIN SOUP

Fill½squash w
⅓c shallot&whlgarlc&oil/
T SweetSpice&brsug h@400°F.
Scoop,puree+6c ZestyStock/
can cocont&tom/
¼c soya&lime.

SOME THINGS ARE MORE
than the sum of their parts.
Rhoda's soup is one of them:
it's both effortless to make and
refined enough for company.

TIP

@RHODACOOK'S SOUP

Finely dice,sauté onion&
celery/T buttr&olvoil;
puree+2½c can tom.
Mix+¼t soda.
Purée, heat+1½c milk/s+p.

SPINACH SOUP

Sauté onion/T oil;
+6c Stock/¼c rice/2T garlc/
t oreg/dash cinn&rdpep&
clove 7m; +bnch spinach 5m.
Puree+2T olvoil&lem/s+p.

TIP

MY PARTNER WAS THE original architect of Twitter, and also this soup, which is nearly as addictive. Use any pears on the firm side of ripe.

@BLAINE'S PEAR & SPINACH SOUP

Sauté shallot/T buttr;
+lb grns&pear/4c Stock.
Simmr8m,puree
+½c gorgonzola/2c milk/
nutmeg&s+p.
Top w walnts.

TIP

THIS FUSION DISH PAIRS strawberries and rasam, a spicy broth from India. Strawberry nectar is in the bottled juice section of supermarkets.

STRAWBERRY RASAM

Brwn t garlc&ging/
2t CurryPowder/shallot/T oil;
simmr+2c strawberrynectar&
ZestyStock/t GaramMasala.
Srv w lime&strawberry.

ROASTED TOMATO & FENNEL SOUP

Mix¼c oil/T garlc&brsug/
c tom&carrot&fennel.
h@325°F; +4c Stock/
t rosemry/bay.
Simmr9m.
Rmv bay,puree,sieve.

TIP

SUNCHOKES, OR JERUSALEM artichokes, are an under-appreciated root vegetable, with a subtle flavor reminiscent of roasted chestnuts.

SUNCHOKE VELOUTÉ

Brwn2T buttr/onion&leekwt&
garlc/3c sunchoke.
Simmr+6c Stock/BqtGrni 20m.
Rmv grni; puree+wtpep/
⅓c crm.

YAM SOUP

Sauté leek&onion/T buttr/
t SweetSpice. Simmr20m
+4c Stock/3c yam/tater/bay.
Rmv bay; puree+½c yogurt/
s+p. Top w tstdpumpkinseeds.

DRESSINGS

TIP **REFRIGERATE ANY EXTRA** dressing for up to a week. Bring to room temperature before using.

CITRUS BUTTERMILK DRESSING

In a med jar, shake ½c buttrmilk/2T lem or lime/¼t dijon&zest/s+p. Yld scant¾c.

@RHODACOOK'S CREAM DRESSING

Whisk⅓c crm/2t sug/T vinegr/ s+p until light.

TIP **THIS UNUSUAL DRESSING IS** great on basic garden salads, or tossed with cold, diced Boiled Potatoes and scallions for a quick potato salad.

GREEN PICKLE DRESSING

In foodproc, blend½c parsly/ 2T caper/T shallot&vinegr/ dillpickle&garlc; slowly +¼c olvoil. Yld¾c.

YOGURT DRESSING

Whisk T olvoil well into
t dijon/¼t salt; +⅓c yogurt/
T lem/wtpep to taste.
Yld½c.

Ⓜ QUICK VINAIGRETTE

In a med jar, mix2T vinegr/
¼t salt/t dijon; +⅓c olvoil.
Shake; +dijon/pep/dash sug
to taste.
Yld¾c.

Ⓥ GARLIC VINAIGRETTE

For strong garlic flavor
+mincdclv to Quick
Vinaigrette.
For a hint +crushedclv to
vinegr~2h; rmv.
Yld¾c.

PEPPER-PARSLEY VINAIGRETTE

In foodproc, blend½c olvoil&
parsly/¼c winevinegr/t dijon
&paprka/½t s+p/⅛t wt&rd
pep&sug.
Yld c.

VINAIGRETTE DE PROVENCE

In foodproc, blend½c olvoil/
¼c rdwine/T basil/t dijon/
¼t HerbesdeProvence/s+p.
Yld¾c.

BALSAMIC VINAIGRETTE

Boil c balsamic/t brsug/garlc;
simmr@med-low~15 m to
reduce by ⅔. Rmv garlc;
whisk+⅔c Olvoil/½t pep/
¼t salt (to taste).

SALADS

TIP

TO DRESS A SALAD, BE AN angel with the salt, a devil with the pepper, a miser with the vinegar, and a spendthrift with the oil.

AVOCADO STRAWBERRY SALAD

Per srvg, lyr c rdlettuce/ sliced½avocado/½c snowpea &mungbeansprout&strawberry. Drizzle w BalsamicVinaigrette.

BACON SALAD

Fry8oz julienedbacon/T olvoil; rmv bacon.
Deglaze+3T cidervinegr; reduce by ½.
Toss+4c greens.
Top w bacon/gruyere/s+p.

BLT SALAD

Spread4pce bread w ¼c mayo.
8m@475°F; cube.
Fry,chop12pce bacon.
Toss all+½c mayo/
3T rdvinegr/4c romaine/
2c cherrytom/s+p.

BIG-BATCH BEAN SALAD

Mix⅓c oil&vinegr&sug/t s+p;
+can lima&kidney&garbanzo/
c gr&ylw bean&celery.
Chill,mix occas>8h.

GREEN BEAN SALAD

Blanch4c beans.
Simmr t tarrgn/¼c vinegr.
Toss all+½c walnt&slivered
shroom/⅓c walntoil/t dijon/
2T parsly/s+p.

FOR BROILED SALAD, USE
your best extra-virgin oil. Tuck
in grapes as best you can;
the presentation is inevitably,
delightfully chaotic.

TIP

BROILED SALAD

Steep¼c vinegr/t tarrgn;
+⅓c olvoil/s+p.
Drizzle on 4heart romaine
stuffed w c slicedgrape.
Top w pecorino.
Broil~30s.

BREAD SALAD

Dice2c bread/c cuke&tom.
Toss w 3T olvoil&balsamc
&basil&onion/T tstdfennelseed/
garlc/salt&wtpep to taste.

HOMEMADE CROUTONS ARE
far better than store-bought:
Rub stale bread with garlic,
then cube and toast for
15m@300°F or in a dry skillet
@med.

TIP

THE EGGS IN THIS SALAD ARE
not cooked. As such, don't
serve to the elderly, immuno-
compromised, or small
children.

TIP

CAESAR SALAD

Mince6anchovyfillet/garlc;
+t grndmustard/½c olvoil.
Whisk+egg/lemon.
Toss l lrg romaine/¼c parm/
3c crouton; +lem/s+p to
taste.

GRILLED CHEESE SALAD

Toss6c greens/3T srcrm&
lem&oil/t dijon/s+p.
Broil4pce baguette w
3T chevre/t olvoil&chopddill/
¼t garlc e.
Top greens.

CHEVRE & BEETS

Steam2lb sm rd&ylw beet
20m; cool,peel,wedge.
Top w whisked
2T olvoil&balsamc/s+p;
+2oz crumbledchevre/
T oreg&tstdnut.

CHICKEN CANTALOUPE SALAD

Mix¼c mayo/2T srcrm&mango
chutney/t dijon/s+p.
Toss+2c melon&cookd
chicken/c celery&apple&
scalion&tstdnut.

ALMOND CHICKEN SALAD

Toss3c dicedcelery&cookd
chicken/c scalion/½c raisin
&slicedalmond&mayo/
¼c oj/s+p.
Chill.
Srv on greens w orangeslices.

COLESLAW

Toss4c grcabbage/2c car/
⅔c Aioli or Mayonnaise/
¼c sug/3T winevinegr/
½t tstdceleryseed/s+p.

RED SLAW

Toss3c rdcabbage/
c rdonion&apple/
½c dill&beetpickle; chill.
Toss+3T olvoil/T vinegr/
½t dijon&tstdcarawayseed/
s+p.

THIS CRUNCHY, SPICY AND
sweet Thai corn salad requires
freshly picked corn, which is
abundant at roadside stands
and markets in Thailand.

TIP

YAM KHAO POT

THAILAND Blend t rdcurry paste/2T cocontmilk&peanut& lime&cilantro/T fishsauce& dryshrimp(opt).
Toss+2c sweetcorn/ ¼c tstdcocont.

TIP

ANY VEGETABLES YOU'D normally serve as crudités will work here, cut as usual or in more refined pieces the size of your pasta shape.

CRUDITÉ PASTA SALAD

Whisk3T mayo&srcrm&lem/ T chive&parsly/s+p/anchovy fillet(opt).
Blanch 3c mixdcrudité.
Toss all+12oz aldentepasta.

AUTUMN ENDIVES

Core,quarter,plate6endive.
Drizzle w whisked 2T walntoil/ T cidervinegr/dash s+p&garlc; +⅓c tstdwalnt&pecorino or bluecheese.

FENNEL & PERSIMMON

Soak T shallot&vinegr/ t orangezest/s+p 30m; whisk+¼c olvoil.
Toss+4persimmon/ slicedfennel; top w ⅓c parsly&parm&tstdnut.

TIP

@KELLAN TRAVELS A LOT, as do I. When we cross paths we cook together, and this salad often makes the menu. Clementines may also be used.

@KELLAN'S FENNEL & POMEGRANATE SALAD

Toss thinslicedfennel/blood orangesegments/pomegranate/ mixd 3T lem&olvoil/s+p.
Top w shavedpecorino.

MANGO AVOCADO SALAD

Compose3c mixdgreens/ slicedavocado/c mango/ T verbena or cilantro; top w whisked 2T olvoil&honey/ T lime/s+p.

KNEADING KALE HAS THE same effect as cooking it, without robbing you of the garden-fresh flavor. Raisins may be used instead of currants.

SERVE THIS FUN SALAD AT a picnic. Use instant ramen, which is already pre-fried; after chilling it becomes al dente. Toss before serving.

RAW KALE SALAD

Stem,chop bnch kale;
knead2m +t salt;
+¼c olvoil&currant/
3T lem/c rdonion&apple.
Top w tstdnuts&cheese.

RAMEN SALAD

Toss3c cabbge/c mung
beansprout/5T peanutoil&
scalion/T soya&vinegr/
pkg ramenspice.
Top w crumbledramen/c
tstdalmond; chill>4h.

CHILI MELON SALAD

Mix4c seededcuke/t salt;
drain~30m.
Boil¼c vinegr&sug&rdonion/
¼t rdpep/rd birdchili; cool.
Toss all+4c watermelon/
s+p.

ORANGE WATERCRESS SALAD

Peel,slice3orange.
Rmv stalks of bnch cress.
Mix T vinegr&mint&parsly/
s+p; whisk+¼c olvoil.
Toss all.

TIP

CREATED IN COLLABORATION
with @buffaloamy, an avid
home cook, gardener, and
mom I met on Twitter, this
crunchy salad is a colorful
delight.

@BUFFALOAMY'S PEA SALAD

Slice rd&ylw&gr bellpep/
¼lb snowpea; blanch30s.
Toss+½c cherrytom/
T balsamc&shallot&olvoil&
lem&dijon/s+p.

TIP

QUINOA IS HIGH IN PROTEIN
and amino acids, and is gluten
free. It may be served plain
like rice, but my favorite way
is Quinoa Salad.

QUINOA SALAD

Toss2c cookd Quinoa/
2T soya/T vinegr&honey/
½t CurryPowder&orangezest
&rdpep/½c bellpep&celery&
waterchestnut&drycranberry.

@RHODACOOK'S GRAPEFRUIT & AVOCADO SALAD

Boil2c h2o; +c quinoa 12m.
Cool,+2T soya&oj/t zest/
T honey&olvoil/c avocado&
grapefruit&celery/s+p.

SPINACH NUT SALAD

Top5c tornspinach w diced
apple/c mixdnut/3T parm.
Toss+whisked 3T nutoil/
T vinegr/½t soya&dijon&dill/
s+p.

TIP

THE BEST WAY TO EAT
summer tomatoes is with a
sprinkling of salt, oil, and
some fresh herbs.

COMPOSED TOMATO SALAD

Slice,overlap4ripetom; sprinkle
w coarsesalt/pep/whisked
3T olvoil/t lem/mincdbasil&
chive.

HORS D'OEUVRES

Quintessentially small in form, but big in flavor and sociability, these offerings will awaken guests' taste buds and leave them anticipating what's to come. They're also an easy way to bring a world of new tastes and textures to the plate, from a piquant melitzanosalata eggplant dip from Greece to the warm flavors of Moroccan baked olives to spicy Asian-style fried tofu.

Dips aside, it's wise to give yourself extra time to prepare hors d'oeuvres, which often rely on careful and well-timed presentation. Preparing basic ingredients in advance will help ensure that these little bites emerge from the kitchen, perfectly hot or cold, just as guests settle in with their first drinks.

DIPS

TIP

SERVE GUACAMOLE AND salsas with tortilla chips, other dips with crackers, flatbreads (eg Focaccia, Pletzel, Kesra) or Herb or Onion Bread.

BABA GHANOUSH

MIDDLE EAST Mash RoastedEggplant flesh+ 3T tahini&lem&olvoil&yogurt (opt)/t salt&garlc. Chill. Srv w flatbread. Yld c.

GUACAMOLE

MEXICO Seed sm hotchili; mash+3T scalion&cilantro/ ½tcumin/2avocado/lime/salt. Srv immed or wraptight. Top w tom&cilantro. Yld c.

Ⓜ HUMMUS

MIDDLE EAST Soak c chickpea>8h. Replace h2o; simmr3h. Drain,puree+⅓c tahini& lem&olvoil/½t garlc&salt/ cayenne to taste. Chill. Yld c.

ⓥ ROASTED GARLIC HUMMUS

Puree RoastedGarlic to taste w Hummus.

ⓥ ROASTED PEPPER HUMMUS

Puree 1 RoastedPepper, such as red bell, Anaheim, or jalapeño w Hummus.

ⓥ MINT HUMMUS

Puree⅓c mint w Hummus.

ⓥ TOASTED SPICE HUMMUS

Stir in skillet@low until fragrant + cuminseed& coriandrseed/¼t pepcorn; grnd. Puree w Hummus.

MELITZANOSALATA

GREECE Charbroil whl eggplant; peel.
Beat+dash salt/garlc;
slowly+¼c olvoil/3T vinegr.
Chill2h.
Srv w pita.
Yld c.

TIP

RAITA IS TRADITIONALLY served with spicy, stewed and grilled dishes.

RAITA

INDIA Grate cuke,press,strain.
Tst t cuminseed@med; grnd.
Mix all+c yogurt/⅓c mint& cilantro/½t salt.
Chill.
Yld c.

TIP

THESE SALSAS ARE ALSO great with Scrambled Eggs, Cheese Omelets, Migas, Easy Chili Rice, Home Fries, and numerous other dishes.

SALSA FRESCA

MEXICO Peel,seed 4tom;
mince+¼c wtonion&cilantro/
1-2jalapeño(seed for milder salsa).
Toss+2T lime/s+p to taste.
Yld c.

SALSA ROJA

MEXICO Boil2c tom/
10–20serranochili/h2o to cvr;
simmr15m.
Foodproc+t garlc/¼c cilantro/
hotliquid as nec/½t oreg&salt.
Yld c.

MANGO RHUBARB SALSA

Very finely dice c rhubarb/
2c mango/scalion/seeded
jalapeño/T cilantro&mint&
olvoil&lime/salt.
Chill.
Yld3c.

SALSA VERDE

MEXICO Husk,broil
lb tomatillo~7m.
Sauté onion&jalapeño/T garlc&
oil; +tomatillo/½c h2o.
Simmr15m; +lime&cilantro&
s+p.
Yld2c.

OLIVE TAPENADE

FRANCE Foodproc c olv/
¼c caper/2T olvoil/t garlc&
thyme/pep.
Yld½c.

SWEET PEA TAPENADE

Puree c SimplePeas/T lem/
pinch zest&salt&cayenne/
¼c pinenut&parm.
Yld½c.

ONE SUMMER STRAWBERRIES
were otherworldly, so I made
a feast of them for friends and
invented this sublime dish.
Mint may replace verbena.

TIP

TARTARE DE FRAISES

Mince lb strawberry/ylwpep/
scalion/¼c alfalfa&verbena;
+3T lem&olvoil/tabasco&
s+p to taste.
Garnish w capers.
Yld 3c.

SMALL BITES

ALCACHOFAS FRITAS, PIMENTOS de Padrón and Patatas Bravas should be served promptly with Romesco or lemon wedges.

ALCACHOFAS FRITAS

SPAIN Peel,stem,halve,rmv choke of 12babyartichoke; cvr w h2o/lem.
Drain,dry,deepfry8m in olvoil; salt.

TO TEST WHETHER OIL IS hot enough (350°F-375°F) to properly deepfry most foods, drop in a cube of bread; it should brown within 60 seconds.

PIMIENTOS DE PADRÓN

SPAIN Rinse,drain,dry lb padrónpep.
Deepfry8m in olvoil; salt.
Eat these tiny peppers stem and all.

PATATAS BRAVAS

SPAIN Cook HomeFries in
olvoil; +coarse salt.
Srv w Romesco.
(These are not patatas bravas
without it.)

TIP

THIS SATISFYING CHEESE MAY
be baked in a shallow tart
pan or in ⅓ PuffPastryDough,
rolled medium-thin. Jam or
marmalade may replace honey.

BAKED BRIE

Cut open 9oz brie; fill
w 2T honey/basil to cvr/
dash nutmeg.
Wrap w 10"PuffPastry(opt).
10m@350°F(just oozing).
Srv immed.

TIPSY BRIE

Rmv rind of 9oz brie;
soak+½c wtwine 8h.
Drain,blend+¼c buttr/
2T brandy/⅛t cayenne&pep.
Top w T brdcrmb&parsly.
Srv w crackers.

CARROT FLAN

Simmr7m 2c babycarrot/
1½c milk/dash nutmeg&
dryging/s+p; cool.
Puree+4egg/½c crm.
Oil/fill4ramekin; 30m@400°F
in bainmarie.
Cool.

CAULIFLOWER BITES

Toss cauliflrflorets/3T olvoil/
2t cumin&garlic/+Curry
Powder/s+p.
Roast on bkgsheet~20m
@400°F., turn 1x.
Srv w Raita.

CHEVRE & POMEGRANATE PORTOBELLOS

Stem/oil4portobello; stuff w
½c chevre/s+p.
Wrap w 4pce prosciutto(opt).
25m@375°F.
Top w pomegranateseed.

EGGPLANT ANTIPASTO

Ribboncut ½RoastedEggplant.
+grnd T garlc&parsly&
mint&basil/½c olvoil;
+¼c olv/2T caper(opt).
Chill24h.
Srv w toast.

GORGONZOLA CROSTINI

Cream⅓c gorgonzola/2T buttr;
+T brandy/½t paprka/pep.
Brwn16sm slices baguette/
T buttr&olvoil; top w cheese.
Srv immed.

KARTOFFELPUFFER

GERMAN Grt,rinse4c tater;
towel-dry well.
Beat egg/2T flr/¼c
mincdonion; toss all.
Deepfry4patties.
Srv w AppleSauce.

WILD MUSHROOMS PROVENÇAL

Mix t garlc/¼c olvoil/
½t thyme&lavender;
+2lb chopdshroom.
Sauté10m; toss+⅓c parsly/
3T lem/½t garlc/s+p.

Ⓜ GEM'S WINE-BAKED OLIVES

Mix in sm bkgdish c unpitd
blkolv/½c rdwine/¼t garlc&
crushedfennelseed/
T olvoil/pep.
20m@325°F uncvrd.

Ⓥ MOROCCAN SPICED OLIVES

Tst,toss t cumin&coriandr
seed/dash rdpep w Gem's
WineBakedOlives before
baking.
Toss~T cilantro&mint&lem.

BAKED PROSCIUTTO & ASPARAGUS

Wrap12lrg aspargus w
18pce proscuitto; put in
buttrdbkgdish.
Top w ¼c mltdbuttr/¾c parm.
10m@450°F.

ONION RINGS

Slice2lrg onion.
Dip rings w mixd ¼c flr/
T milk/egg/½t bkgpdr&s+p;
+flr or cornmeal.
Bake15m@450°F or
deepfry~3m.

PARSNIP SOUFFLÉ

Brwn T buttr&flr.
+c milk; +c parm/
mashdparsnip/3yolk/
⅛t nutmeg&s+p.
Fold+3whipdeggwt.
Fill6ramekin.
30m@375°F in bainmarie.

THIS POLENTA IS PORRIDGE-
like, creamy, and smooth, with
a crisp cheesy top—much like
a savory crème brûlée. Serve
right out of the oven.

TIP

PARMESAN POLENTA

Boil2c h2o/c milk/¾t salt;
slowly+¾c medcornmeal.
Simmr25m@low; +2T buttr/
garlc/s+p.
Fill4ramekin,top w ¼c parm e.
Broil.

QUESO FUNDIDO

MEXICO In oven-safe skillet
brwn½lb shroom&rdonion/
T oil; +2mincdchipotle/
2c mozz or quesillo.
7m@350°F.
Srv w tortillas.

TIP

IF YOU HAVE A PERFECT bunch of radishes, it's worth making or seeking an excellent, complexly flavored butter for this match made in heaven.

TIP

TRY THIS SAUSAGE AS PART of a classic ploughman's spread of bread or crackers, pickles, cheese and lemon-sprinkled apple or pear slices.

RADISHES WITH BUTTER & SALT

Pipe3T softbuttr onto 12coldhalvdradish; +smidgen fleurdesel e. Srv immed.

@TEEANDTOAST'S RAREBIT

Stir,mlt@low2T buttr/c cheddar/⅛t dijon&pep; beat+2yolk.
Brwn c shroom/t butter.
Top 4pce toast w shroom& sauce.

ABERDEEN SAUSAGE

SCOTLAND Foodproc c bacon& beef&bread/egg/
T worces&parsly/s+p.
Tie in muslin,steam2h.
Unwrap,dredge w c brdcrmb.
15m@300°F.

ALMOND-CRUSTED TOFU

Cut lb extra-firm tofu 1"x2".
Mix ½c grnd&sliced almond/ s+p/¼c starch.
Dredge tofu; deepfry~4m.
Srv w soya.

SPICY TOFU

Cut lb extra-firm tofu 1"x2"; cvr8h w pureed 3lemgrass&garlc&shallot/ chili/3T soya&lime.
Dry; dredge w strch/s+p.
Deepfry~3m.

SUMMER TOWERS

Cut12slices RoastedEggplant/
2lrg tom/8oz mozz.
Whisk2T lem/¼c olvoil/s+p.
Lyr4servings 3x w eggplant/
tom/dressing/basil/mozz.

STUFFED ZUCCHINI BLOSSOMS

Sauté⅓c zuke&onion&
tom&rice/T olvoil;
+T mint&lem/s+p.
Stuff8blossom; +½c Stock/
T olvoil&tompaste.
Cvr,simmr25m.

TIP

I'VE MADE THIS PATÉ COUNT-
less times and guests adore
it. Nutritional yeast has a high
umame quotient. The recipe
fills three 6-oz ramekins.

VEGETABLE PÂTÉ

Sauté yam&celery&
carrot&onion/¼c olvoil/¼t
thyme&sage&cayenne&s+p.
Puree+1–3T lem&soya&flr&
nutri yeast/c sunflrseed.
h@350°F.

VEGETABLES

Vegetable dishes often get short shrift, and they often deserve it. Thoughtlessly seasoned overcooked green beans are pretty commonplace. But it's not difficult to make distinctive and scrumptious vegetable preparations—it just takes a little thought and care. And considering there is a greater variety of organic and local produce on the average supermarket shelf nowadays than there once was at most farmers' markets, what better time to celebrate the most simple, seasonal and elemental part of our diet?

The flavor profiles in this section are a little lighter than in others, so as to highlight the essence of each central ingredient. On that note, use the highest-quality, freshest vegetables possible. For example, cauliflower noisette and new eggplant parmesan don't bury their namesakes in heavy sauces; they let their unique characters through. Pair these dishes with meat or fish, put several together for a vegetarian meal or just serve one with a green salad and some crusty bread. You won't be disappointed.

SIDE DISHES

BOILED ARTICHOKES

Trim,peel stems (they're delicious); cvr w cold h2o/ T olvoil/hvyplate to sink. Simmr~20m until knife pierces base easily.

ⓜ STEAMED ARTICHOKES

Trim,peel stems.
Place on wire rack over boiling h2o/t salt or CourtBouillon.
Cvr-h@low(+h2o as nec).
Dry5m@300°F.

ⓥ MAPLE LEMON ARTICHOKES

Srv4SteamedArtichokes w pureed ¼c mltdbuttr&lem/ 3T maple/t mustard&drying/ s+p.

SERVE ROASTED OR STEAMED
Asparagus with a Flavored
Butter, Citrus Sauce or any
Pesto thinned with olive oil.

THESE BEAN RECIPES WILL
work with any type of fresh
bean, such as runner, yellow,
French, Blue Lake or Dragon's
Tongue.

ROASTED ASPARAGUS

Trim~16; peel lrg.
Coat w ¼c olvoil/½lemzest
&juice; +T grndhazelnut/
seasalt&pep.
Broil to blister, 2-4m.
Srv w buttr.

Ⓜ STEAMED ASPARAGUS

Trim~16; peel lrg.
Boil3c h2o/t buttr/¼t salt;
+aspargus in steamerbasket.
Cvr to tender~3m for sm/
5m med/7m lrg.

Ⓥ ASPARAGUS NOISETTE

Place SteamedAsparagus in
warm dish.
Stir⅓c buttr@med to lgtbrwn;
top aspargus.
Srv immed.

Ⓜ FRESH GREEN BEANS

Boil6c h2o/2T salt&vinegr;
+lb beans 3m.
Drain,toss+any FlavoredButtr.

Ⓥ AIOLI GREEN BEANS

Toss FreshGreenBeans+
½c Aioli/2T parsly/s+p.
Srv immed.

Ⓥ GARLIC GREEN BEANS

Sauté4garlc/¼c olvoil to
golden; toss+FreshGreen
Beans/s+p 2m.

Ⓥ MEDITERRANEAN
GREEN BEANS

Toss FreshGreenBeans+
whiskd 2T rdvinegr/3T olvoil/
t tompaste&lem&oreg/s+p.
Top w ¼c crumbledfeta&
olv(opt).

Ⓥ RAITA GREEN BEANS

Toss FreshGreenBeans+
½c Raita.
Top w GaramMasala.
Srv immed.

TIP

THESE GREEN BEANS BELONG
to a category of Greek cuisine
called *ladera,* or "oily." Serve
in bowls with crusty bread on
the side.

FASOLAKIA

GREECE Sauté2c onion/
⅓c olvoil; +lb grbean/
2c crushedtom/slicedlater
(opt)/pinch sug/¼c parsly&
mint/s+p.
Simmr15m.
Srv w feta&lem.

ZIPPY GREEN BEANS

Sauté5m@low 2 T garlic&oil;
I 3c grbean/slicedrdbellpep/
T lem&Stock/½t sug/t thyme/
dash cayenne 5m+; s+p.

QUICK ORANGE BEETS

Shred lb beet; +T Mustard
Butter/¼c oj/s+p.
Cvr5m@med to tender; uncvr
to evaporate liquid.

@BITTMAN'S BEET RÖSTI

Grate2lb beets; mix+
t salt&rosemry/⅓c flr.
Brwn3T buttr; +beets.
Form round,brwn.
Slide to plate; flip,brwn
2nd side.

SPRING BEETS

Sauté2m 4grtdyoungbeet/
T buttr/s+p; +3T h2o/
cvr~3m until tender.
Mix+T buttr&parsly&lem/t
dijon&shallot.

Ⓜ COOKED BEETS

Either bake+¼"h2o in
cvrddish~30m@375°F,
or steam 30m@med.
Test tenderness,cool to peel.

ⓥ SALT & PEPPER BEETS

Chop lb CookedBeets; heat in pot+T buttr/2T lem/½t s+p.

ⓥ HONEYED BEETS

Chop lb CookedBeets; + 2T mixd honey&lem/ T mltdbuttr.
Stir/simmr to coat; s+p.

TIP

MY PARTNER'S AUNT LINDA is an amazing gardener who grows a lot of beets. Her recipe can convert almost anyone into a beet-green lover.

LINDA'S BEET GREENS

Rinse,chop bnch beetgrns.
Sauté,stir+T buttr/s+p to wilt(+h2o if dry).
Cvr5m@low(stir occas); +2m uncvrd.
Srv w vinegr.

PIQUANT BROCCOLI

Blanch,dry lb broccoli.
Fry2garlc/2T oil.
Rmv garlc; +2mincdanchovy fillet/¼t rd&blk pep 2m.
Stirfry all; top+3T balsamc.

A HYBRID OF BROCCOLI AND gai lan, broccolini is the best of both, with nutty-flavored florets on long, tender stems.

TIP

HOT ORANGE BROCCOLINI

Sauté¼c olvoil/2garlc&shallot/ orangezest/¼t rdpep&s+p; +lb broccolini 1m; cvr3m+ juice from orange/T balsamc.

CREAM-BRAISED BRUSSELS SPROUTS

Lightly brwn lb quartered brusselssprout/3T buttr/ ¼t salt; +c crm.
Cvr30m@low.
Uncvr; +T lem/s+p.
Simmr3m.

JUNIPER CABBAGE

Boil6c h2o/T salt; +
5c shreddedcabbage 4m.
Drain,rinse.
Crack5juniperberry,sauté5m
+T buttr/leek; +cabbage.
Cvr10m@low; s+p.

SWEET CARROTS

Scrub4c carrot; boil or steam
+sprg parsly to tender.
Toss w 2T mltdbuttr/T brsug/
¼t salt.

BRAISED CARROTS

Mlt2T buttr; boil+2lb carrot/
h2o to cvr/T honey&vinegr/
½t salt/sprg thyme/dash pep.
Cvr15m@low(+h2o if dry).

HERB-ROASTED
CARROTS

Toss2lb carrot/2T olvoil&h2o/
s+p/5whlgarlc/sprg thyme
in bkgdish.
Cvr35m@400°F(+2T h2o if
dry); +5m uncvrd to brwn.

Ⓜ MILK-POACHED
CAULIFLOWER

Boil c milk/3c h2o/½t salt;+
florets&stem of med cauliflr.
Simmr5m to easily pierced.
Srv w buttr.

Ⓥ CAULIFLOWER NOISETTE

Stir¼c buttr@med to lgtbrwn.
Gently toss w MilkPoached
Cauliflower offheat; s+p.

Ⓥ QUICK CURRIED
CAULIFLOWER

Mix,sauté3T buttr&lime&
shallot/T CurryPowder/t garlc.
Gently toss+MilkPoached
Cauliflower/¼c cilantro&
tstdcashew.

Ⓥ CELERIAC GRATIN

Sauté,simmr2c tom/onion/s+p.
Sauté6c celeriac/2T buttr;
cvr+½c h2o>9m.
Brwn¼c buttr&flr;
slowly+2c milk.
Lyr4x.
20m@400°F.

CELERY GRATIN

Chop bnch celery.
Simmr+3c Stock 30m;
rmv to bkgdish.
Reduce c Stock 5m;
+3T buttr/¼t dijon.
Cvr celery; +½c parm/pep.
Broil.

SLOW-BRAISED CHARD

Toss2bnch chopdchard/
⅓c olvoil&h2o&cilantro/
c onion/t paprka&garlc&salt.
Cvr45m@low(+2T h2o
if dry); s+p.

STUFFED CHARD

Sauté c chandstem&
onion&apple/2T oil;
+t caraway&paprka&
garlc/2c carrot&parsnip
20m@med; +lem&s+p.
Stuff8leaves.
Simmr+c Stock 9m.

COLLARDS

Rmv stalk,chop3lb collard;
+to 6c boiling h2o/
⅓lb smokedpork/
whlchili&garlc.
Simmr20-50m to taste; drain.
Srv w hotsauce/s+p.

SIMPLEST CORN ON THE COB

Boil8c h2o/2t sug(opt);
simmr+4shuckedears~6m.
Drain; s+p.
Srv w buttr(plain or flavored).

GRILLED CORN

Shuck all but innermost husk
of 4ears; snip tips.
Broil or grill 10m.
Turn until charred.
Rmv char,husk.
Srv w buttr/s+p.

SUCCOTASH

Kernel4corn,rsv juice.
Heat3T buttr/corn/2c cookd
limabean/s+p; boil+
cornjuice/Stock to cvr.
Simmr7m; +T parsly/
½t paprka/s+p.

EGGPLANT PARMESAN

Dredge¾"slices
RoastedEggplant w egg,
c brdcrmb.
Brwn+2T buttr.
Float in 3c simmrring
TomSauce; +c parm.
Broil; +T parsly.

SPICED-BUTTER EGGPLANT

Stir@low until fragrant
¼t grndmustard&cumin&
coriandr; +3T buttr/garlc.
Top RoastedEggplant.
Srv w RicePilaf&parsly.

TIP

THIS EGGPLANT DISH IS EASY
to make and easy to become
addicted to. I serve it with
crusty Kesra, Fresh Pasta,
Brown Rice or Plain Risotto.

ZAALOUK

MOROCCO Mix2c tom&peeled
eggplant/½c tompaste/t cumin
&paprka&garlc&sug&s+p.
Cvr h@350°F.
Mash w ¼c lem&mint.

SEARED ENDIVE

Toss lb quarteredendive(or
radicchio/escarole)/3T olvoil/
s+p; cvr~h.
Brwn+T olvoil@med-high
~2m/side.
Rmv,fan open,s+p.

STEAMED FENNEL

Boil bay&fenneltops;
l quarteredfennel in
steamcrbasket.
Cvr20m@med-low.

FENNEL PIE

ITALY Lyr2c bread/¼c milk/chopd steamedfennel&boiledegg/ 2c grtdcheddar; rpt.
Top w ¼c parm/T dottedbuttr. 45m@375°F to brwn.

TIP

THIS DISH MAY BE PREPARED with any Asian greens, such as bok choy, choy sum or a mix. Use baby varieties or chop larger greens.

SESAME GREENS

Fry3m T sesoil&olvoil& ging&garlc; +4c greens/ ¼c h2o 3m.
Rmv garlc&ging; +T soya/ dash sug.
Top w sesseed.

Ⓜ SIMMERED KALE

Trim tough stem off 2bnch kale.
Boil8c h2o/T salt; +kale 5-30m to desired texture.
Strain(press lightly); srv w buttr/s+p.

Ⓥ KALE & BREAD

Brwn2c dicedbread in oven or skillet.
Toss½+hot SimmeredKale; top w rem ½.
Srv immed w vinegr or hot sauce.

CARAMEL KALE

Chop lb kale; steam stems 9m.
Brwn2pce chopdbacon(opt); stir20m@low+2T buttr/ 2c onion/t salt&sug; +kale/ ¼c wine.
Cvr3m.

POACHED LEEKS

Halve4leek.
Brwn+2T buttr; +½c wtwine3m.
Simmr+2c Stock/BqtGrni ~15m; rmv leek to dish.
Reduce sauce by ½; +T wine.
Top leeks.

CRANBERRY PARSNIPS

Mix¼c brsug&cranberry&
mltdbuttr/4c peeled&juliened
parsnip/½t dijon&pep.
Cvrd20m@350°F;
+20m uncvrd.
+T chive.

TIP

IF YOU'RE COOKING WITH
larger, mature peas (which
taste quite starchy raw) add
a teaspoon of sugar and
increase simmering time to
5 minutes.

SIMPLE PEAS

Shell2lb youngfreshpeas;
+to boiling h2o/t salt.
Simmr~m to just tender.

PEAS WITH PROSCUITTO & MINT

Blanch2c peas
Toss+whisked T olvoil/
½t vinegr/s+p; +2T mint/
oz bitesize prosciutto.

SPRING MIX

Shell lb pea&fava.
Steam¼lb fiddleheadferns
4m; +pea3m;
+¼lb aspargustip&
snowpea/fava2m.
Top w buttr/s+p.

STUFFED PEPPERS

Brwn onion/2c shroom/2T oil.
Mix+c cookdrice&feta/
T parsly&mint/s+p.
Stuff4bellpep; top w
2c TomSauce.
40m@350°F(baste3x).

Ⓜ BOILED POTATOES

Mix2lb sm tater/T salt/
8c cold h2o; boil.
Simmr@med-low to
just tender.
Cut in half; toss+3T buttr&
chive(opt)/s+p.

ⓥ AROMATIC BOILED POTATOES

+citruszest/2T mincdherbs w buttr in BoiledPotatoes.

ⓥ SAVORY BOILED POTATOES

Heat3T buttr to foaming;
+mincdshallot to brwn.
+T rosemry or sage.
Sub for buttr in
BoiledPotatoes.

SALT POTATOES

Cvr2lb sm tater w h2o;
+½lb salt(yes, really).
Boil to fork-tender; drain.
Srv brushed w buttr.

MY FRIEND'S GRANDMA ("mormor" in Danish) first served me this salty, savory and sweet dish. Resting the potatoes helps the sauce to stick.

TIP

MORMOR'S POTATOES

DENMARK Boil2lb babytater tender; peel,rest30m.
Stir5T sug@med to just brwn;
+5T buttr to dissolve.
Stir+tater~10m.

ROASTED POTATOES

Toss4c cubedtaters/2T oil/
T lem&HerbesdeProvence or
ItalianMix/mincdgarlc/dash
cayenne&s+p.
Turn occas~h@400°F.

FRENCH FRIES

Peel(opt)4lrg flourytater;
cut in ¼"lengths.
Cvr w h2o/ice; chill30m.
Dry. Deepfry7m.
Cool on papertowel 10m.
Deepfry5m; s+p.

TIP

IN QUÉBEC, NO WINTER passes without poutine, a literal "mess" of French fries, cheese curds and brown gravy. Diced Gouda can replace curds.

TIP

SOME NIGHTS I USE PACKAGED foods such as hash browns, out of convenience or nostalgia, and in homey dishes like this one from a friend of mine.

POUTINE

CANADA Top thick-cut FrenchFries w c freshcheese curds&Gravy/s+p. Srv immed.

CRACKED POTATOES

GREECE Hit15sm tater to crack. Fry10m in 2c olvoil. Rmv oil; +5T wtwine/ 2T coriandr/T lem/s+p. Cvr+toss@high until dry.

TURMERIC POTATOES

Sauté onion/¼c oil; +T salt/ t turmeric/½t cayenne~m; +2lb sm tater sliced½"/ ¼c h2o. Stir,cvr10m(+h2o as nec).

JEAN'S HASH BROWNS BAKE

Mix2lb frozenhashbrn/c cheese &onion/can celerysoup/ ½c srcrm&friedbacon(opt)/ s+p. Top w c frenchfriedonion. 35m@350°F.

POTATO CRUNCH

Grt,rinse4c tater; press dry w towel. Mix+⅓c cheese&mltdbuttr/ c onion/t garlc/2T parsly. Cvr45m@400°F; +20m uncvrd; s+p.

SCALLOPED POTATOES

Boil~2m 4c milk/3lb sliced tater/t salt&garlc/c leek/BqtGrni.
Lyr3x w lgt dusting wtpep &nutmeg&parm/dots buttr. h@375°F.

TIP

THIS CRUNCHY-TENDER DISH comes from my partner's dad, Rick, whose skills range from rink to barbecue. Use the grill for best results.

@HOCKEY'S POTATOES

Fry5c tater/2T buttr&oil in ironpan or foil on bbq.
Top w scalion/T ItalianMix &garlc/s+p/c cheddar.
Broil or grill crisp.

TIP

CHOOSE FLOURY RUSSETS for fluffy mashed potatoes, or use waxy potatoes, such as Yukon Gold, if you want a chunkier texture.

Ⓜ MASHED POTATOES

Mix2lb flourytater/4c h2o; boil.
Simmr20m@med-low
Peel,mash; beat+⅓c buttr/c lgtcrm/t salt/pep.

Ⓥ GARLIC MASHED POTATOES

Squeeze cloves from bulb RoastedGarlic into MashedPotatoes; beat well.

COLCANNON

IRELAND Peel,boil lb tater; chop,steam½lb kale.
Mash all w s+p.
Brwn onion/2T buttr; +mash all @med-high.
Brwn btm; turn in pces.

PUMPKIN CURRY

Brwn c onion/T oil&garlc; +4c peeldpumpkin 5m.
Simmr5m+c ZestyStock; +cancocont/t currypaste 5m.
Srv w lime&cilantro.

WINE-BRAISED RADISHES

Sauté shallot/thyme/2T buttr;
+20 radish/s+p/¼c wtwine/
h2o to cvr.
Simmr3m; rmv to bowl.
Reduce juice 5m; top radish.

ROOT BRAISE

Slice,lyr yam&turnip/2parsnip
&tater/2c kale&collard/
3c cheddar/s+p.
Slowly+c Stock.
Simmer partly cvrd45m;
broil+½c cheddar.

SHIITAKES & BOK CHOY

Blanch,quarter~lb bokchoy.
Slice2c shiitake; +T oil&garlc.
Sauté3m; +bokchoy/
¼c Stock/T soya/t sesoil/s+p.
Stirfry3m.

SPINACH & MUSHROOMS

Brwn2T buttr/2c shroom/
s+p; rsv.
In pan +T buttr&garlc/
lb spinach/s+p to wilt.
Toss all.
Srv w toast or tossed w pasta.

IN THE FOLLOWING DISH, ANY
orange winter squash such as
butternut, acorn, kabocha or
pumpkin may be used.

TIP

SPICY SQUASH & CARROTS

Brwn onion/T oil; +T garlc&
ging&honey/½t CurryPowder&
cinn/s+p; +c Stock/2c squash
&carrot.
Cvr,simmr20m; +3T oj.

BAKED TOMATOES

Halve,core4lrg tom;
place in buttrdbkgdish.
Top+¼c scalion/s+p/
chopdbasil/⅔c brdcrmb.
Dot w buttr.
10m@350°F.

SCALLOPED TOMATOES

Peel,slice8tom.
Lyr3x w mixd 2c brdcrmb/
mincd onion/3T oil/¼t s+p.
Top w ½c parm or pecorino.
25m@375°F.

STUFFED TOMATOES

Cut off top,scoop4lrg tom.
Mince flesh/shallot/8olv;
mix+2c cookdrice/3T mayo&
pinenut/T olvoil/s+p.
Fill tom.
20m@400°F.

TURNIP GRATIN

Brwn onion/2T buttr;
+c Stock/¼c crm.
Reduce by ½; s+p.
Thin slice 2turnip&tater;
lyr4x w sauce.
Top w 2c tornbread.
h@375°F.

EASY YAMS

Scrub4lrg yam.
Put in dish+¼" h2o;
seal w foil.
~h@375°F.
Mash+¼t cinn&s+p/
2T maple&buttr&lem.

DON'T BE ALARMED BY THE amount of filling for four skins; the skins in both of these Twice-Baked Yams recipes are meant to be overstuffed.

A FUN AND EASY DISH, THIS creamy all-vegetable stew can either be served as a main course with rice (I recommend Coconut Rice) or as a side.

MAPLE TWICE-BAKED YAMS

Pierce5yam; 40m@350°F
on rack to tender.
Scoop,mix flesh+½t thyme/
2T srcrm&maple/cayenne/
s+p.
Fill4skin; 5m@375°F.

CHIPOTLE TWICE-BAKED YAMS

Pierce5yam; 40m@350°F
on rack to tender.
Scoop,mix flesh
+T chipotle&sauce/
2T lime&srcrm/s+p.
Fill4skin; 5m@375°F.

PEANUT BUTTER STEW

Brwn t cumin&coriandr/
garlc&chili&onion/T oil;
+c yam&tater&bellpep&zuke.
Simmr15m+can coconut&
tom/½c soya&peanutbuttr.

GRAINS & BEANS

FOR FLUFFY RICE, RINSE first, add a little lemon, and don't stir while cooking. When done, place cloth between pot and lid to absorb steam.

LONG-GRAIN WHITE RICE

Rinse2c long-grain wtrice; drain in sieve.
Boil+2½c h2o; cvr15m@med-low; +15m offheat.

LONG-GRAIN BROWN RICE

Rinse2c long-grain brrice; drain in sieve.
Boil+4c h2o; skim any foam.
Cvr40m@low; +15m offheat.

PARBOILED RICE IS MORE nutritious than regular rice because it's been processed by boiling in the husk. It's also firmer and less sticky.

PARBOILED WHITE RICE

Rinse2c parboiled wtrice;
drain in sieve.
Boil+2½c h2o; cvr20m@low;
+15m offheat.

PARBOILED BROWN RICE

Rinse2c parboiled brrice;
drain in sieve.
Boil+4c h2o; cvr35m@low.
Stir.
Cvr,simmr10m; +10m offheat.

TIP

USE A PLATTER TO FOLD AND fan-cool the rice. For sushi rolls, spread on nori seaweed sheets, fill along one edge, roll up and slice.

SUSHI RICE

JAPAN Warm,mix ¼c
ricevinegr/T sug&mirin/t salt.
Rinse,drain 2c sushirice.
Boil+2c h2o;
cvr5m@med,9m@low.
Fold vinegr&rice; fan.

TIP

A SOUTHEAST ASIAN STAPLE, short-grained sticky, or glutinous, rice is often rolled into bite-size balls and dipped into sauces and curries.

STICKY RICE

SOUTHEAST ASIA Soak3c
glutinous rice/6c h2o 24h.
Drain,steam in basket or
clothlined sieve 25m.

TIP

THIS AROMATIC RICE GOES well with spicy Pumpkin or Snow Pea & Shrimp Curry, or tropical fruit drizzled with Honey Syrup.

COCONUT RICE

THAILAND Rinse,drain
2c jasmine rice; boil+
1½c h2o/c can cocont/t salt.
Cvr15m@low; +10m offheat.

RISI E BISI

ITALY Sauté onion/3T olvoil&
pancetta; +c arborio&peas.
+5c Stock to just cvr
(+extra as nec).
Simmr20m; +½c parm/
T buttr/s+p.

BOMBA IS A MEDIUM-GRAIN
white rice, aka calasparra. You
can sub arborio. This entree
is usually made in a wide,
shallow pan.

Ⓜ RISOTTO

ITALY Heat,stir c arborio/
T buttr&oil@med;
+½c wtwine;
+½c hot Stock until absorbed.
Rpt Stock ~8x over~24m.
Mix+½c parm/s+p.

ALSO TRY MIXING SIMPLE
Peas, diced Roasted Eggplant,
Steamed Fennel or cooked
root vegetables into Risotto
toward the end of cooking.

PAELLA

SPAIN Sauté onion/¼ c olvoil;
+2c bomba/3T garlc&tompaste;
+⅛ t saffron/4c Stock.
Top w c shrimp&clam
(or pea&tom).
20m@450 °F; + lem/s+p.

EASY CHILI RICE

Mix T oil/¼c onion/t chilipdr
in ricecooker; +c rice~7m;
+1½c tomjuice/½c pea&
corn/t oreg.
Cvr until shut off(or 15m@low).

Ⓥ RISOTTO WITH SHALLOT & HERBS

Sauté c shallot or onion w the
buttr&oil; +¼c mild(eg basil/
dill) or T strong(eg rosemry/
sage) herbs w rice.

PECORINO IS ITALIAN SHEEP'S
milk cheese; pepato is pecorino
studded with peppercorns,
delivering a punch to pastas,
salads and risottos.

Ⓥ CREAMY CORN RISOTTO

Stir in c cornkernel/
pureed c crm&corn
@ end of Plain Risotto.
Pecorino pepato recommended
instead of parm.

Ⓥ ENDIVE RISOTTO

Stir in ½c crm/½chopd
SearedEndive
@ end of Risotto.
Top e bowl w fanned Seared
Endive/T parsly&parm/lemslice.

Ⓥ BEET RISOTTO

Puree c CookedBeet w
the Stock.
Sauté shallot/T ging&garlc
w rice.
When tender mix+½c diced
CookedBeet before the parm.

Ⓥ BARLEY RISOTTO

Sauté onion&garlc w
the buttr&oil; sub c barley
for arborio.
When tender mix+¼c
parsly&lem before the parm.

THREE-GRAIN RISOTTO

Sauté onion&garlc w the
buttr&oil.
Sub⅓c arborio&barley&quinoa
for arborio; +½c parsly w
the parm.

RICE PILAF

MIDDLE EAST Soak c
arborio~30m.
Sauté shallot/2T pinenut&
currant&buttr; +rice 3m.
Boil+1½c Stock/s+p;
cvr20m@low.

TECHNICALLY TINY PASTA, couscous comes in two common forms: instant, which takes minutes to cook, and regular, which is slower but tastier.

QUINOA

Boil2c h2o/dash salt;
stir+c quinoa.
Cvr,simmr15m@low;
+10m offheat.
Fluff.

COUSCOUS

Rinse2c regular couscous.
Drain15m,fluff.
Steam20m uncvrd.
Rmv to plate; top w mixd
c h2o/t salt&oil.
Fluff,rest10m.
Steam20m+.

QUINOA PILAF

Brwn⅓c onion&carrot/
T buttr&oil; +t garlc/
½t s+p&turmeric/
c quinoa 2m.
Boil+2c h2o.
Cvr,simmr15m.
Fluff+2T cilantro&mint.

FENNEL COUSCOUS

Brwn onion/T buttr&garlc.
Simmr9m+T tompaste&
Harissa/3c h2o&fennel/s+p.
Cvr c hotliquid&instant
couscous 5m.
Toss w fennel.

PIQUANT LENTILS

Simmr c lentildupuy/4c h2o/
t salt/garlc tender~15m.
Drain; heat +2T sherry&olvoil
&scalion/½t garlc&anchovy/
¼t rdpep&thyme.

TIP

DALS ARE INDIAN LENTIL
stews. When cooked, red
lentils have a fall-apart,
smooth texture; brown ones
are firmer.

BROWN DAL

INDIA Fry T oil/t cumin;
+c onion/T garlc&ging&
CurryPowder.
Simmr20m+c brlentil/3c h2o.
Mash+2T lem&buttr.
Srv w cilantro.

RED DAL

INDIA Simmr,cvr3c h2o/
c rdlentil/T tamarind h.
Fry¼c oil/T CurryPowder/
½t cayenne&salt; +c onion/
T garlc.
Mix all/lime&cilantro.

HURRY CURRY

Put2c veg/½c onion&lentil
&brrice/1½c Stock/T sug&
tompaste&CurryPowder/
t tstdcumin in ricecooker until
shut off(or 45m@low).

BLACK, PINTO AND KIDNEY beans are all great in chili. Top with sour cream, scallions and sharp cheese. Don't omit both beef and beans.

BASIC DRIED BLACK BEANS

Boil3m,soak3h
c blkbean/4c h2o.
Replace h2o,simmr h; drain.
Brwn t garlc&cumin/
T buttr&oil; +beans/
⅓c tomjuice/s+p.

CHILI

Brwn lb grndbeef(opt);
+onion&anaheimpep/
2T garlc&oil; +3c tom/
T chilipdr/t grndcoffee&
cumin&chipotle/c cookd
bean(opt).
Simmr40m.

VEG CHILI

Sauté onion/T oil; +T garlc&
grndcoffee&chilipdr/c shroom/
bellpep&carrot&celery;
+3c tom&cookdbean/
T worces&soya&lem/s+p.
Simmr h.

ADZUKI BEANS, ALSO KNOWN as red beans and popular in Asia, are the fastest-cooking dried bean, requiring only 20 minutes when pre-soaked.

Ⓜ JAMAICAN RICE & BEANS

Cvr,simmr½c adzukibean/
2c h2o 30m; +c can cocont&
wtrice/onion&garlc/¼t thyme
&s+p/hotchili.
Cvr,simmr20m.

ⓥ BROWN JAMAICAN RICE & BEANS

Sub c short- or
long-grain brrice.
Tst in dry skillet for deeper
flavor(opt).
Increase h2o to 2⅔c.
Simmr~40m.

ESPINACAS CON GARBANZOS

SPAIN Brwn c wbread/T garlc/
c olvoil; grnd; +t cumin
&paprka&s+p.
Simmr+T vinegr/c h2o/
3c spinach&cookdchickpea
20m.

ⓥ GREENS, RICE & BEANS

Stem,slice2c kale;
dice grbellpep&scalion.
Stirfy+2T oil/t ging&garlc;
+2c wt or br JamaicanRice
&Beans/s+p.

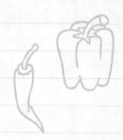

NOODLES & PASTA

Noodles and pastas are my favorite foods for their global reach and sheer adaptability. Whether savored at the incredible, heady-smelling food stalls in China's Sichuan Province or in the understated kitchens in the hills of Tuscany, they are ever-familiar, yet infinitely reinvented—and always very satisfying.

Noodle and pasta doughs must be kneaded with even more vigor than yeast breads and, in general, they are labor intensive but also fun to make, so help in the kitchen is a big plus. Hand-pulled and cut noodles have an appealing texture, but you may also use a machine, which is almost always the best choice for pasta. Once they are perfectly al dente, they may simply be tossed with some butter browned with fragrant herbs, the makings of a rich alfredo sauce or a vibrant pesto.

On the other hand, there are plenty of choices for heartier, more involved dishes, such as classically rich macaroni and cheese, rustic summer lasagna, and scrumptious meat ravioli. But no matter which type of noodle or pasta you prepare, remember these two things: Heavily salt the water and don't cook beyond al dente.

FRESH NOODLES & PASTA

AFTER BOILING FRESH NOODLES, USE IMMEDIATELY IN RECIPES such as Beef Noodles, Laghman, Noodle Stir-Fry, or Pumpkin Curry.

TO DRY FRESH NOODLES OR PASTA, FLOUR AND DRAPE FOR A day over a pasta rack, a wooden chair back or a clothes rack. Boil 10m to cook.

TOSS COOKED FRESH OR DRY PASTA WITH ANY PESTO, VELOUTÉ, Cheese, Onion or Tomato Sauce (sieved for a more refined dish).

FRESH NOODLES

CHINA Knead2c flr/egg/
t salt/½c h2o.
Quarter,roll12"x4"; cut4"x½".
Cvr30m.
Pinch,stretch from center
to dbl.
Boil6m.
Yld~lb.

ⓂFRESH PASTA

ITALY Knead hard
¾c semolina&flr/2egg/T olvoil;
wrap~h.
Quarter,roll thin,hang<10m.
Cut as desired/
rest on flr.
Boil~3m.
Yld~lb.

ⓋARUGULA PASTA

Blanch4oz arugula(or other
delicate/flavorful greens/
herbs); wring,mince.
Knead w eggs/oil in
FreshPasta.

USE FLOURY POTATOES SUCH
as Russets to make gnocchi.
In order to cook properly,
the gnocchi should be cut
no larger than the size of a
thimble.

TIP

EASY GNOCCHI

Steam,peel,sieve lb tater.
Knead+¼t salt/⅔c flr.
Squeeze,snip from pastrybag
to 8c simmring milk/t salt;
~m to float.
Buttr.

SPÄTZLE

GERMAN Mix c flr/2egg/
¼c milk/T mltdbuttr/
⅛t nutmeg&s+p.
Fill ricer>¾,squeeze
into boiling h2o.
Simmr30s.
Srv w cheese&buttr&Gravy.

NOODLE DISHES

BEEF NOODLES
Stirfry¾lb slicedflanksteak/
T peanutoil; +t garlc&rdpep&
sug; +c basil/¼c h2o/T soya&
lime&fishsauce.
Toss w aldenteFreshNoodles.

KASHGARI PEOPLE ARE
descendants of ancient
Turkic tribes. Folk dishes
like Laghman fuse Chinese
and Muslim flavors with
northern rusticity.

TIP

LAGHMAN
KASHGAR Brwn½lb lamb/
onion/T garlc/t cumin&
coriandr/3T oil; +2c bellpep/
3c tom/s+p 6m@med;
+T ricevinegr.
Top aldenteFreshNoodles.

MANGO YAKISOBA
Stirfry¼t thyme/garlc/2T oil/
c leek&shroom; +c mango/
½t rdcurrypaste/¼c lem/
2T soya&mint.
Toss+14oz aldentesoba.

NOODLE STIR-FRY

Brwn½lb slicedpork/3T oil;
+T garlc&ging; +aldente
FreshNoodles/¼c soya&
scalion/2T ricevinegr/t rdpep&
brsug&sesoil/s+p.

RICE NOODLES COOK FOR
a shorter time than wheat
noodles. Buy in larger or
Asian grocery stores and
cook according to package
instructions.

TIP

PAD THAI

Stirfry8oz chicken(or tofu)/
3T oil; +8oz cookdflatrice
noodle/½StirFrySauce;
+btnegg/2c sprout.
Srv w peanut&lime.

CILANTRO PRAWN NOODLES

Stirfry8peeledprawn
(or shrimp)/T olvoil&lime/
t garlc/s+p 2m.
Toss8oz cookdricenoodle/
¼c AsianPesto; top w prawn.

RICE-NOODLE PRIMAVERA

Toss SpringMix @low
+9oz cookdricenoodle/
Citrus Sauce.
Top w scalion&lime.

UDON CURRY

Brwn c onion/T oil;
+4c pumpkin 5m.
Simmer5m+c Stock/
chili&garlc; +can cocont/
t rdcurrypaste 5m.
Srv w lb udon/lime&cilantro.

PASTA DISHES

TIP GENERALLY, FINE SHAPES GO well with light sauces, chunky shapes with hearty/chunky sauces and twisty shapes with creamy/rich sauces.

MARCELLA HAZAN'S CARBONARA

Slice,fry c bacon; +T garlc.
Simmr+¼c wtwine.
Beat 2egg&yolk/½c parm.
Toss+lb aldentespagheti/
bacon/½c parm/pep.

FAVA-TOMATO TOSS

Brwn onion&garlc/2T olvoil;
+2c peeled tom&favas.
Toss+3c arugula/
aldentepasta(pref
ArugulaPasta)/s+p.
Top w parm.

CONCHIGLIETTE & PEAS

Fry½c pancetta; +⅓c olvoil/
mincd chili&garlc/2c peas 5m.
Toss w 3c aldente
conchigliette/¼c parsly/s+p.
Srv w lem&parm.

CONTRARY TO POPULAR belief, authentic Fettuccine Alfredo does not have any cream in it. But the real thing is so divine, you won't miss it.

FETTUCCINE ALFREDO

ITALY Boil12oz(pref fresh) fettucine to aldente.
Boil¾c pasta h2o/½c buttr; toss well+pasta/3c parm until creamy.

DINER-STYLE FETTUCINE ALFREDO

Simmr¼c buttr/½c crm/ t garlc; +c cookd shrimp or shroom(opt).
Toss+12oz aldentefettuccine.
Top w parm&pep.

PINK PEPPER FETTUCINE

Rinse,slice2lb beetgrn&stem.
Sauté T garlc/¼c olvoil; +grns.
Cvr7m@low; toss
+12oz aldentefettucine/
T pinkpep/½c parm.

FAVA CHICKEN GEMELLI

Brwn lb chopdchicken;
+c peeledfava.
Keep warm.
Toss OnionSauce/
12oz aldentespinachgemelli.
Top w chicken&fava mix.

TRY THIS LASAGNA WITH Fresh Pasta sheets. You can also enrich it with Bechamel, browned ground meat, lentils, or more vegetables.

SUMMER LASAGNA

Slice eggplant&zuke/4oz mozz;
oil,s+p,broil veg.
Lyr3x c TomSauce/
cookdlasagnanoodle/veg/mozz/
basil,+½c sauce&parm.
h@325°F.

ANCHOVY PARMESAN LINGUINE

Sauté¼c anchovyfillet&buttr.
In hotsrvgdish, toss lb aldente linguine/½c parm/wtpep/anchovymix.
Srv w parm&pep.

MAC & CHEESE

Undercook3c macaroni.
Brwn¼c flr&buttr; +2c milk/½t dijon&pep/c cheddar.
Mix+pasta/top w c cheddar&tornbuttrdbread.
10m@400°F.

TIP

NUDI ARE TENDER ORBS OF ravioli filling, "nude" of any pasta. Serve with melted butter, perhaps browned with herbs, and Parmesan and pepper.

NUDI (NUDE RAVIOLI)

ITALY Mix c ricotta/egg/salt&wtpep/⅓c flr.
Chill.
Roll~20 t balls,toss w flr.
Boil5m; rmv w slottedspoon.
Srv on sauce.

SPINACH NUDI

Sauté,chop bnch babyspinach.
Mix+c ricotta/egg/T parm/s+p.
Roll~24 t balls,toss w flr.
Boil3m; rmv w slottedspoon.
Buttr.

SAFFRON ASPARAGUS ORZO

Brwn c orzo/garlc/T buttr; +¼t saffron&s+p/2½c Stock.
Cvr9m@low;
+2c aspargus 3m.
Fold+½c parm.
Srv w parm.

PUMPKIN ORZO

Sauté shallot/3T sage/T buttr;
+1½c Stock/c milk.
Simmr; +1½c can pumpkin/
s+p~10m.
Mix+c aldenteorzo/3T parm.

VEGETABLE ORZO

Sauté onion&garlc/3T oil;
+diced zuke&eggplant 8m;
+c orzo/diced celery&carrot/
2c tom/c h2o/s+p.
h@350°F.
Top w parm.

WHITE BEAN PASTINI

Boil c soakedwtbean h.
Fry t rosemry&cumin&garlc/
T oil; +bean/T tompaste/
h2o to cvr.
Simmr+c pastini to aldente.

PENNE ARRABIATA

ITALY Sauté mincd onion&
med-hotchili/¼c olvoil.
Simmr+2½c tom/
¼t rd&blk pep.
Toss,heat+10oz
aldentepennc/¼c basil.

MANGO PENNE

Fry garlc&chili/½c scalion/
T ging&sesoil.
Simmr+3mango/2T soya&lime/
¼t rdpep/¼c can cocont/
lemgrass.
Toss+10oz aldentepenne.

ALTHOUGH YOU DISCARD THE
browned fennel seed, sage
and garlic in the Penne Rosé,
they leave the oil with a
wonderful flavor and aroma.

TIP

PENNE ROSÉ

In 3T oil brwn,discard t fennel
seed&sage&garlc; +c onion&
pea 5m; +12oz aldentepenne/
5T crm&parm/T tompaste&
lem/t pep/½t salt 3m.

TIP

TO MAKE RAVIOLI, PLACE filling between ~3" squares Fresh Pasta, seal w h2o and butter before saucing. Wonton wrappers work quite well, too.

TIP

I SERVE THE FOLLOWING ravioli with browned butter, herbs, parmesan and pepper; a Pesto and olive oil; or any Tomato Sauce and basil.

GREEN RAVIOLI

Sauté2c spinach/T garlc&oil;
+c ricotta/½lem&zest/s+p.
Spoon~t on
~12pastasquares,top,seal.
Boil 4m.
Srv w SpringMix.

MEAT RAVIOLI

Sauté lb grndmeat/2T buttr.
Brwn+garlc/T parsly;
+3T brdcrmb&parm/s+p.
Spoon~t on
~12pastasquares,top,seal.
Boil 4m.

SWEET PEA RAVIOLI

Mash c SimplePeas/egg/
T sherry/t mint&parsly/s+p.
Put~t on ~12pastasquares,
top,seal.
Boil 4m.
Srv w crm&parm&s+p.

TIP

PUMPKIN RAVIOLI IS PARTIC-ularly good when tossed with sage sautéed in butter, drizzled with Crème Fraîche, then dusted with fresh nutmeg.

RICOTTA RAVIOLI

Mix c ricotta/egg/s+p/⅓c flr/
nutmeg/T mildherbs.
Spoon~t on ~12pastasquares,
top,seal.
Boil 4m.

PUMPKIN RAVIOLI

Sauté shallot&garlc,
+½c can pumpkin&ricotta/
T lem/t zest&brsug/
⅛t nutmeg/s+p.
Spoon~t on ~12pastasquares,
top,seal.
Boil 4m.

RIGATONI BEER RAGOUT

Brwn c onion&chorizo/
T ItalianMix&garlc&oil;
boil+3c tom/2c beer&
bellpep&celery.
Cvr h@low; +10oz rigatoni
to aldente.

TAHINI BROCCOLI SPAGHETTI

Cook12oz whtspagheti firm,
then aldente w 2c broccoli.
Toss+2T sesoil&tahini&soya/
½c olv/s+p.

SKILLET SPAGHETTI

Brwn½c onion&shroom/
T garlc&olvoil.
Boil+2c tom/½c TomSauce&
h2o/T tompaste&ItalianMix/
s+p; +10oz raw spagheti.
Simmr~20m.

MEATBALLS

Mix½lb grndbeef/egg/
⅓c parm&brdcrumb/
T garlc&basil&parlsy&oil/
t dijon/s+p.
Form balls<2".
Simmr>30m in desired
sauce or soup.

SLOWGHETTI

Cvr Meatballs w 6c TomSauce/
c rdwine in slowcooker.
Cvr5-7h@low; +12oz raw
spagheti ~h+.

SPINACH SPAGHETTI

Brwn T garlc/¼c olvoil;
+5c spinach.
Cvr 3m.
Toss+12oz aldentespagheti/
s+p; +T olvoil/3T parm.
Top w parm.

MAINS

Whatever the occasion, humble or fine, there's a main course here that suits your needs. Whether it be the homey Irish stew or chipotle pork, elegant moules marinées or chicken roulade, you'll find flavors that are full yet sophisticated, comforting yet still exciting. Hopefully, you'll enjoy and revisit them all.

At this station in the planet's history, it seems worth reminding everyone that our oceans are depleted of many once-abundant fish, and that poultry and livestock are not commonly farmed with traditional decency, nor even with the ambition to produce quality food. If you're interested in organic produce, I urge you to further embrace the true cost of good food by seeking out traditionally farmed meats and poultry—the results will be well worth it—and to purchase only sustainable sea creatures. To that end, my fish and seafood recipes generally call for the most sustainable catches. In the cases where the type of fish is left for you to choose, please do so wisely.

FISH & SHELLFISH

DARK FISH (E.G. SALMON/CHAR/BASS/MACKEREL/TUNA) ARE best grilled/baked, light fish (e.g. cod/halibut/tilapia/sole) steamed/poached/panfried.

USE SKINNED ½"-1" FILLETS IN RECIPES, UNLESS OTHERWISE indicated. Your fishmonger should skin fillets upon request.

DEEP-FRIED FISH

Dredge4fillet w ½c milk,
c brdcrmb/T parm(opt)/
¼c strch/½t s+p/⅛t cayenne,
deepfry brwn~2m@325°F
(don't crowd).
Rmv to paper.

Ⓜ PAN-FRIED FISH FILLETS

Dredge4fillet in ½c milk,
mixd s+p/c flr.
Heat T oil&buttr to
shimmering; +fish 2-3m/side
@med-high to just flaky.

Ⓥ FILLETS MEUNIÈRE

Put PanFriedFish in warmdish.
In hot pan+2T buttr to
foaming; whisk+lrg lem/
¼c parsly/s+p.
Top fish.
Srv w lemwedges.

Ⓥ FILLETS WITH HOLLANDAISE

Srv PanFriedFish with
HollandaiseSauce.

TIP

POACHED LIGHT FISH MAY BE
served simply with lemon or
Hollandaise; Poached Dark
Fish pairs well with Béarnaise
or Choron Sauce.

POACHED LIGHT FISH

Simmr½c wtwine/
4c CourtBoullion(or h2o);
+4lgtfillet.
Cvr w buttrdparchment.
Cook below simmr to
flaky~8m on stovetop.

POACHED DARK FISH

Buttr dish,4fillet; +shallot/
½c wtwine/CourtBoullion
(or h2o) to cvr.
Cvr w buttrdparchment;
30m@375°F to flaky.

ORANGE BUTTER FILLETS

Mix t salt/½t pep/2T oj&
zest/3T mltdbuttr.
Top⁄lgt or drk fillet;
+ ¼t nutmeg.
15m@450°F or grill until
flaky.

VERMOUTH FILLETS

Simmr¼c buttr&vermouth/
T lem&tompaste/s+p in
skillet; +4lgtfillet.
Baste@high until flaky.
Rmv; +½c crm to pan.
Top fish.

WHOLE FISH SHOULD BE scaled, gutted and rinsed. They are cooked when a knife slides easily into the center and is warm against your lower lip.

A FISHERMAN IN TRINIDAD shared this recipe with me. It's how he prepares his choice catch at the end of the day. Use any white-fleshed fish.

WHOLE BAKED FISH

Buttr dish,fish; +¼c wtwine& herbs(opt)/s+p.
Cvr w foil 9m@400°F +6m/lb(baste2x) to flaky.
Srv w drippings/lemwedges.

FISH STEW

Sauté onion/¼c olvoil;
+T garlc 2m;
+½c parsly&tom.
Simmr+¾c wtwine/ 2c FishStock;
+2lb lgtfillet 10m.
Break up fish; +½t oreg.

FISHERMAN'S DINNER

TRINIDAD Cvr4lgtfillet w lime&zest/¼c onion&tom/ t garlc&ging 20m.
Sear; +¼c h2o,cvr3m.
Uncvr,glaze w T ketchup&oil.

MOROCCAN BASS

Flr/s+p4fillet.
Brwn2m/side+3T oil/t cumin.
Put in warmdish.
In pan sauté2c tom&chickpea/2T preserved lem&cilantro.
Top fish.

CHAR WITH OLIVES

S+p,brwn4fillet skindown
+3T oil~3m; turn m.
Put in warmdish.
Sauté2sprg rosemry/T oil;
+½c olv/2T balsamic&lem.
Top fish.

TIP

BUY TIGHTLY SHUT, FRESH-
smelling mollusks. Before
cooking, soak in saltwater
20m, then scrub to remove
any dirt and sand.

HALIBUT & CLAMS

Sauté4c shroom&leek/
½c buttr.
Boil+3c FishStock;
+4fillet/20clam.
Cvr7m@low; +T basil/
s+p(only srv openclam,
cook shut3m+).

QUICK JAMBALAYA

Sauté2c shrimp/¼c buttr/
c onion&shroom&bellpep&
celery/2c tom/t paprka/
dash cayenne;
+2c anycookdrice/s+p.
h@350°F.

MISO-ROASTED MACKEREL

Mix¼c wtmiso&honey/
T sesoil&soya.
Cvr8fillet 20m.
Brwn skindown+3T oil~3m@
high.
5m@350°F to flaky.
Srv w lemwedges.

Ⓜ JULIA CHILD'S MOULES

Sauté shallot/garlc/T olvoil/
bay&thyme; +2lb mussel/
⅔c wtwine.
Cvr,shake,5m@high to
open(discard shut ones); s+p.

Ⓥ JULIA CHILD'S MOULES MARINÉES

Shell,mix JuliaChild'sMoules/
¼c olvoil/3T parsly/2T shallot/
T vermouth&lem.
Chill30m.
Srv in shells(opt).

STEAMED SABLEFISH

Grt,strain2"ging.
Mix juice+t soya&sug&h2o;
cvr4fillet 20m.
Steam in parchment over
boiling h2o+c scalion~4m.
Srv w rice

SALMON HASH

Dice,brwn3tater/onion&
bellpep; +15m@med.
Fold,heat+c chopped
smokedsalmon/
T chive&lem/s+p.
Srv w mixd ½c srcrm/
T chive&lem.

TIP

MAPLE WOOD IMPARTS AN aroma to whatever is cooked on it, as does cedar. Use a plank of untreated wood small enough to fit on the grill.

MAPLE SALMON

Soak mapleplank 3h.
Cvr4fillet w ½c maple/
t FiveSpice/2T oil/s+p.
Put on plank in cvrdgrill
15m@med to flaky.
Srv w lemwedges.

MISO SALMON

Whisk¼c brmiso/T oil&sug&
mirin&sake(opt); +4skin-on
salmonsteak.
Marinate1-8h.
~10m@400°F+broil
to brwn.

TERIYAKI SALMON

Marinate4salmonfillet w
2T soya&mirin&brsug/t oil&
garlc&ging&paprka>1h.
Baste/grill~20m.

SIMPLE SEASONED SHRIMP

Boil2lb peeldshrimp/h2o
to cvr/t salt/5celerytops/
T PicklingSpice until
shrimp are pink.
Drain.
Srv w buttr.

SNOW PEA & SHRIMP CURRY

Heat2T oil&CurryPowder
to fragrant.
Stirfry+2c peeldshrimp 4m;
+2c pea&can cocont/s+p.
Simmr2m; +¼c lime&cilantro.

TOMATO SHRIMP

Sauté½c bellpep&onion&
celery&tom/¼c buttr;
+4c tom/bay;
+2lb peeldshrimp.
Cvr,simmr15m,+mixd c h2o/
T strch/¼t cayenne&
s+p~5m.

PECAN TILAPIA (OR SOLE)

Dredge4lgtflllet w flr,buttrmilk,
½c grndpecan&brdcrmb/s+p.
Brwn+T oil~2m/side to flaky.
Srv w limewedges.

CHICKEN

PINEAPPLE CHICKEN

Brwn lb chopdchicken/2T oil;
+2c mixdveg&pineapple/
T garlc&ging.
Mix+¼c sherry&pineapjuice/
2T ketchup&sug/T strch 3m.

CHICKEN PAPRIKASH

Brwn4breast/2T buttr;
+onion/T paprka;
+c tom&bellpep&Stock.
Simmr30m; mix
+2T srcrm/t flr.
Srv w buttrd FreshNoodles/
s+p.

FOR JUICY CHICKEN, SOAK IN
heavily salted water for an
hour; pat dry. Cook until a
meat thermometer inserted in
thickest parts reads 165°F.

TIP

40 CLOVE CHICKEN

Brwn8pce chicken/s+p/
2T olvoil; +40peeldgarlc/
t oreg/¼c olvoil&celery&
wtwine/2T sherry/chopdlem.
Cvr h@350°F; +9m uncvrd.

UNFRIED CHICKEN

Dip8pce chicken in milk,
mixd c grndcornflake/
T onion+garlcpdr/
t oreg&pep&chili.
Chill.
Cvr40m@350°F;
+30m uncvrd.

TIP

USE SKINLESS, BONELESS
breasts and pound with the
flat side of a meat mallet
between wax paper sheets.

CHICKEN PARMESAN

Pound4bonelessbreast¼";
dredge w c brdcrmb/s+p.
Brwn+T oil&buttr.
Add to 3c simmring
TomSauce; +c parm.
Broil; +T parsly.

CHICKEN DIANE

Pound4breast¼".
Brwn+T oil; rsv warm.
Whisk in pan @med
3T chive&lime&parsly&
brandy/2t dijon.
+¼c Stock,T buttr.
Top chicken.

ORANGE CHICKEN

Brwn8pce chicken/¼c oil;
+c. oj&wtwine/¼c raisin&
almond/t ging/s+p.
30m@350°F,drain,reduce
sauce by ½,whisk+T buttr.
Heat all.

MARCELLA HAZAN'S ROAST CHICKEN WITH LEMONS

Bruise,stab2whl lem.
Stuff in~4lb whlchicken,
tie shut,s+p.
h@350°F(turn1x); 120m
breastup@400°F.

I LOVE THIS DISH FOR ITS simplicity, flavor and stellar presentation: Slicing reveals colorful interior spirals.

SKILLET CHICKEN TASTES even better with aromatic sauces, made in the same pan. Serve over plated meat or add chicken to skillet and coat.

CHICKEN ROULADE
Pound4skinlessboneless breast<¼".
Top w ¾c CreamCheese/ ¼c soaked,chopdDriedTom/ s+p; roll,toothpick,buttr.
20m@400°F.
Slice.

Ⓜ SKILLET CHICKEN
Brwn4breast/2T oil 2m/side;
+2c Stock.
Cvr,simmr15m.
Drain stock,rsv.
Brwn chickn+t oil/s+p 3m/side.
Rsv in warmdish.

Ⓥ CAMEMBERT SAUCE
Deglaze+¼c rsvdstock.
Simmr+½c crm&mincdleek;
+½c camembert to mlt.
Whisk+5T srcream&vermouth/ s+p.

Ⓥ CHOCOLATE ROSEMARY SAUCE
Sauté onion.
Deglaze+c rdwine;
+c rsvdstock/bay.
Reduce5m; +2T drkchoc& cocoa/½t rosemry/s+p.

ⓥ GARDEN SAUCE

Sauté c bellpep&eggplant&
zuke&shroom.
Simmr+2c tom/t garlc/
3T basil&parsly&rdwine/
s+p~10m.

ⓥ GRAPEFRUIT
TARRAGON SAUCE

Sauté shallot.
Deglaze+c rsvdstock.
Reduce5m; +dlcedgrapefruit/
T honey&tarrgn&buttr/s+p.

ⓥ PARSNIP GREEN-APPLE
SAUCE

Brwn2c parsnip/T oil.
Deglaze+c sherry.
Reduce5m; +c rsvdstock/
¼t thyme&cardamom/
2c gr apple.

ⓥ THAI SAUCE

Sauté shallot/t chilipaste/T oil.
Deglaze+c rsvdstock;
1 ½c can cocont/lemgrass/
s+p.
Srv w cilantro&limewedges.

TURKEY

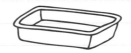

LOOK TO THESE RECIPES FOR AN ABUNDANT YET SIMPLE holiday meal. Most of these recipes feed 9-12 people. Don't forget the Cranberry Sauce.

BUY LB OF TURKEY PER GUEST. FRESH IS BEST; RESERVE EARLY for holidays. Thaw frozen in fridge 2 days if 5-8lb, 3 days 9-12lb, 4 days 13-16lb.

EACH RECIPE STUFFS A 9–12LB TURKEY. MAKE A ½ BATCH FOR 5–8lb, 1½ batch for 13–16lb. Make Stuffing and Gravy with Light Turkey Stock.

STUFFED TURKEY

Rmv giblets(use in Turkey Stock),rinse,pat dry(+inside). Lightly stuff main/neck cavities. Skewer-shut neck; cross,tie legs.

FRESH HERB STUFFING

Sauté4c onion/⅔c buttr; +loose⅔c mixdherbs. Offheat+btnegg/loose10c wtbread/1½c TurkeyStock/ s+p.

CHOPPED OR WHOLE TOASTED nuts make delicious textural additions to stuffings. Try hazelnuts, almonds, or pecans or roasted chestnuts.

TIP

FENNEL & NUT STUFFING

Sauté2c onion&fennel& celery&apple&shroom/ 2T SavorySpice&buttr; +loose8c wtbread/ c TurkeyStock&lstdnut.

HARVEST STUFFING

Sauté onion&celery&apple &carrot/c shroom/3T buttr; +2T SavorySpice&garlc. Offheat+btnegg/loose8c wtbread/c TurkeyStock/s+p.

LET THE ROAST TURKEY REST for 15 minutes before carving and use the time to prepare either Gravy or Fancy Gravy.

TIP

ROAST TURKEY

Put StuffedTurkey on roastrack; baste every 30m@325°F 3-3½h for 5-8lb; 3½-4h for 9-12lb; 4-6h for 13-16lb until thigh>165°F.

TURKEY PIE

Brwn in ironskillet ¼c buttr&onion; +¼c flr& peas; +c Stock/t oreg/s +p; +3c dicedRoastTurkey. Top w rolled ½PuffPastry. 20m@450°F.

THIS VEGETARIAN DISH IS quite beautiful, a darkly glazed, sesame-speckled dome hiding ¼ of any Stuffing (made with Vegetable Stock).

TOFURKEY

Mash2lb firmtofu/
t SavorySpice&
nutriyeast&salt.
Pat bowlshaped in
clothlinedsieve,chill>6h.
Stuff,turn onto bkgpan,glaze.
h@400°F.

TOFURKEY GLAZE

Whisk⅓c sesoil/¼c soya&
oj/2T brmiso/T honey/
½t dijon&honey&orangezest.
Glaze Tofurkey 3x; top 3rd
glaze w T sesseed.

CHOPS & STEAKS

MANCHEGO LAMB CHOPS

Brwn8lambcutlet/
s+p/2T olvoil~2m/side;
+4halvedtom.
Top w c grtdmanchego/
3T basil&parsly/t garlc.
10m@425°F.

TIP

THIS LUSCIOUS DISH WAS
invented by the ingenious chef
Vikram Vij, of Vij's restaurant
in Vancouver.

VIKRAM VIJ'S LAMB CHOPS

Mix¼c sweetwine/
¾c GrainMustard/t s+p.
Cvr4lb frenched
lambchops~3h.
Grill~2-3m/side.
Srv w FenugreekCurry.

CHIPOTLE PORK

Cvr lb ½"strips porkloin/
¼c brsug/T chipotle&sauce/
t salt&garlc&chilipdr 30m.
Broil or grill 3m/side@high.
Top w cilantro.

LEMON PORK CHOPS

Dredge4chop in flr/s+p.
Brwn2T oil; put in bkgdish.
Boil2T lem/½c h2o&ketchup/
T brsug; cvr chops.
45m@350°F.

TENDER STEAK CUTS (FILET
mignon/rib-eye/T-bone/
tenderloin) can go right on the
grill; tougher ones (flank/rump/
sirloin) are best marinated.

REFRIGERATE TOUGH CUTS
4-8 hours in Chermoula or
Lemon-Herb or White-Wine
Marinade. Bring to room
temperature and pat dry
before cooking.

Ⓜ GRILLED STEAK

Buttr,s+p1½"steaks.
Sear@high on grill 2m/side;
@med~m/side for rare,
2m med, 3m well-done.
Rest 5m; s+p.

Ⓜ STOVETOP STEAK

Heat T oil shimmring;
s+p,sear1½"steaks
(2"apart)~40s/side.
Cook@med~2m/side for rare,
3m med, 4m well-done.

Ⓥ BIFTEK À LA BÉARNAISE

Serve any Steak with
Béarnaise Sauce.

Ⓥ BLUE CHEESE STEAK

After turning any Steak, top
e w mixd 2T bluecheese/t
buttr&chopdtstdwalnl/s+p.
Broil briefly to bubble.

TIP

MY FRIEND @NIKETE SHARED
this mouth-watering dish. The
abundant olive oil and salt
form a fine sauce with the
meat juices.

BIFTEK À LA PARRILLA

ARGENTINA Cvr4steak/
½c olvoil~h.
Rmv,+2T coarsesalt.
Sear slde@high;
+2m@med for rare,
3m med, 4m well-done.
Turn,rpt.

ROASTS

TIP

IN THE TWO RECIPES BELOW, "butterfly" means to cut almost through the loin lengthwise, open like a book, season and tie shut at 2" intervals.

TUSCAN PORK

Boil,cool3T salt&sug/
4c h2o; +2lb bonedloin.
Chill8h.
Butterfly w mixd 2T garlc&
rosemry&sage&olvoil/s+p.
~40m@350°F(turn4x).

PRUNE PORK

DENMARK Simmr15pitdprune
+h2o 10m.
Butterfly2lb bonedloin w
prunes/¼c parsly/s+p.
Brwn+3T buttr; +c h2o.
Cvr2h@325°F(+h2o as nec).

PRUNE PORK GRAVY

Deglaze roastpan w c Stock.
Strain; +Stock to yld2c.
Whisk@med ¼c buttr/½c flr;
slowly+¼c milk/stock.
Simmr thick; s+p.

POT ROAST

Brwn,rmv2lb rumproast/
T oil; +2c onion&celery/
c turnip&tater.
Cvr5m; top w roast/BqtGrni/
c BeefStock/¼c rdwine/s+p.
Cvr2h@325°F.

TIP

ROAST BEEF IS RARE AT 125-
130°F, med at 140-145°F,
and well-done at 150-155°F.
Allow 1 rib or 2 pounds of
boneless meat per 2 servings.

PRIME RIB ROAST

At roomtemp, s+p/buttr
2-3rib primeroast; slit,stuff
w 2clv slicedgarlc(opt).
15m@425°F;
+40-50m@350°F to desired
doneness.

TIP

TO TIE BONELESS ROAST,
secure butcher's twine around
one end with 4 feet excess.
Lasso around the roast and tie
snugly at 2" intervals.

ROAST FILET OF BEEF

Rmv all fat; tie compactly.
Brwn+2T buttr/s+p;
flambé+2T brandy.
Roast on roastrack
25-35m@400°F to desired
doneness.

TIP

BEFORE CARVING, ALLOW
roast to "rest" about 15
minutes in open oven so meat
will be juicier. Note that temperature will rise by about 5°F.

HORSERADISH ROAST

IRELAND Tie,s+p4lb sirloin,
cvr w mixd T horseradish&
GrainMustard/¼c yogurt.
15m@425°F; +h
cvrd@325°F to desired
doneness.

SERVE BEEF ROASTS WITH
Gravy, Grain or Cranberry
Mustard, Horseradish Cream
or Béarnaise Sauce, and
Yorkshire Pudding on the side.

THIS SANDWICH WAS
requested by @cookthink;
it makes something exciting
out of leftover roast beef. Let
people top theirs to taste.

YORKSHIRE PUDDING

ENGLAND Mix@high
c milk&flr/2egg/salt.
Brush muffinpan w oil;
preheat @400°F.
Quickly+batter; bake gold/
puffed.

CEMITA MILANESA

MEXICO Dredge4pce
RoastBeef in btnegg,
c brdcrmb/s+p.
Deepfry3m.
Srv e on sesameroll w
avocado&onion&panela
cheese&Salsa.

GROUND MEATS

TIP

GOLABKI MEANS "LITTLE pigeons" in Polish, describing the fatness of these parcels. Finely diced mushrooms may be used in place of the beef.

TIP

SUBSTITUTE GROUND PORK or ground turkey for the ground beef in any of these variations, if you like.

GOLABKI

POLAND Sauté onion/T garlc/ 2T buttr; +t paprka/s+p/ c grndbeef; +c cookdrice. Stuff~8cookdcabbageleaf; +4c TomSauce. Cvr~h@400°F.

Ⓜ HAMBURGERS

Mix lb grndbeef/c bread/ ⅓c milk&onion/egg/ ½t grndmustard&s+p. Oil hands,form4patty. Sear@high; +5m/side @med(or grill8m/side).

ⓥ HERB BURGERS

For mild herbs (parsly/basil/dill)+T fresh or t dry; for strong (rosemary/sage/thyme) +t fresh or ¼t dry to Hamburgers mix.

ⓥ CHEESE-STUFFED BURGERS

Form e Hamburger patty carefully around ~2T cheese (chevre/cheddar/blue). Don't press patties while cooking.

ⓥ ONION BURGERS

Increase onion to ½c. Brwn+T buttr; +to Hamburgers mix +2T instantonionsoup.

ⓥ GARLIC PARSLEY BURGERS

Sauté T garlc&buttr&parsly (or other mild herb); +to Hamburgers mix.

ⓥ HOT BURGERS

+3T tompaste/T garlc& cilantro/t lem&hotsauce/ 2-4mincdseededjalapeño to Hamburgers mix.

ⓥ WALDORF BURGERS

Dice,mix2T apple&celery& walnt&grape/T mayo. Form e Hamburgers patty around 2T.

ⓥ BACON BURGERS

Fry4pce bacon crisp; +to Hamburgers mix +t thyme.

ⓥ MEATLOAF BURGERS

Sub TomSauce for milk in Hamburgers; +T worces& ketchup/t garlc&thyme& brsug to mix.

ⓥ SLOPPY JOE BURGERS

Sub¼c ketchup/2T h2o for
milk in Hamburgers;
+T brsug/¼c bellpep/
t garlc&ylwmustard to mix.

FRITO PIE

In bkgdish lyr2c fritos;
½c onion&cheddar; 2½c chili;
c fritos; ½c onion&cheddar.
20m@350°F.
Srv w any Salsa/srcrm/lettuce.

SHEPHERD'S PIE

Brwn lb grndmeat;
+2c onion&carrot/
c celery&peas;
+ mixd T worces/
⅓ c steaksauce&BeefStock/
s+p.
Top w 3c MashedPotatoes.
40m@375°F.

BUSY SHEPHERD'S PIE

Brwn2c grndbeef.
Toss w lb mixdfrozenveg/can
shroomsoup/s+p; top w
3c MashedPotatoes.
25m@400°F.

SLOPPY JOE BALLS

Simmr2c TomSauce/t
mustard&chilipdr&brsug.
Mix egg/2T brdcrmb&onion/
2c grndbeef/s+p.
Roll12; 15m@350°F.
Top w sauce.

TOAD IN THE HOLE

ENGLAND Beat bubbly 2egg/
c milk&flr/s+p.
Brwn4sausage/2T oil.
Preheat grsdsqpan;
+sausage&batter.
9m@450°F; +20m@375°F.

STEWS

TIP

FOR BEEF STEW, USE 1" cubes of economical chuck/round cuts. Their muscular toughness transforms into a wonderfully toothsome texture.

BEEF STEW
Fry,rmv lb stewbeef/
T flr&CreoleSpice.
Sauté onion&garlc/
T oil; +can beer/2carrot&tater/
bay/t worces&thyme&s+p.
Cvr,simmr2h@low.

TIP

AFTER COOKING THESE dumplings in any Stew, Bœuf Niçoise or Goulash, you can put the pot under the broiler 2-3 minutes until they're golden.

CHEDDAR DUMPLINGS
Cut c flr/⅓c buttr/¼c aged cheddar/T chive/t dijon/s+p;
mix+¼c h2o.
Roll~8balls.
Float in simmring stew~30m.

BOEUF NIÇOISE

Brwn⅓c bacon/2lb stewbeef;
+2c carrot&onion/T lem&
garlc/can tom/BqtGrni/s+p.
Cvr2h@325°F(+h2o if nec);
+¼c parsly&blkolv.

IN THIS DIVINE STEW, USE
Beef Stock and lean stew beef.
Lardons are diced pork fat;
blanch 10 minutes before use
Chianti may replace pinot.

TIP

JULIA CHILD'S BOEUF BOURGUIGNON

Brwn,rmv½c lardon,
2lb beef,carrot&onion.
Flr,s+p. 8m@450°F; +2c pinot
&Stock/T tompaste/BqtGrni.
Cvr3h@325°F.

FOR GREAT STEW, PLACE
parchment under the
casserole's lid for a tight seal.
If sauce is thin after cooking,
strain, then simmer to reduce.

TIP

JULIA CHILD'S MUSHROOM & ONION BOEUF GARNISH

Brwn,rmv½lb shroom/
2T buttr@high.
Brwn20pearlonion/T buttr&oil;
+¼c h2o/BqtGrni.
Simmr30m.

GOULASH

HUNGARY Brwn3c onion/
¼c buttr; 2lb stewbeef; t salt
/T paprka/3T tompaste&h2o.
Cvr,simmr~2h(+h2o if nec);
+½c srcrm.

TIP

IN EPIC POLISH POETRY, hunters are described eating and singing of this tangy-sweet, mixed-meat stew, often served with potatoes and bread.

BIGOS

POLAND Fry c smokedbacon;
+2c stewbeef/onion&bay;
+2c tom&cabbage&
sauerkraut/½c rdwine&
pitdprune/t allspice&pep/
4kielbasa.
Cvr3h@low.

TIP

QUINTESSENTIALLY IRISH, coddle is a cheerful, satisfying pork stew in a thick, tasty broth of apple cider. Serve with Soda Bread.

DUBLIN CODDLE

IRELAND Brwn lb
bacon&sausage; +sliced
onion&tater&carrot/3garlc/
mixd bnch herbs/3c cider/s+p.
Cvr,simmr3h. Srv w parsly.

GUINNESS STEW

IRELAND Brwn,rsv2lb
chuck/3T oil.
Brwn4c onion&rootveg;
+T garlc&brsug&flr.
Boil+2c beer&BeefStock/beef/
bay/s+p.
Cvr3h@300°F.

TIP

VARIATIONS OF MAFÉ (PEANUT stew), some with spinach, yam or corn, exist across West and Central Africa. Serve with Harissa.

MAFÉ

ETHIOPIA Brwn c onion/
lb stewbeef/T oil.
Boil+¼c peanutbuttr&
tompaste/2c BeefStock;
+2c carrot/thyme&bay/s+p.
Cvr~h@low.
Srv w rice.

HONEY TAGINE

MOROCCO Brwn lb chopdlamb/
2T buttr/t dryging&turmeric&
cinn&s+p; +2c onion&carrot
9m; +c stock/3T honey/
9pitdprune.
Cvr‑h@400°F.

LEMON TAGINE

MOROCCO Brwn lb chicknpces/
3T buttr; +2c onion&tater/
3T lem&parsly/⅛t saffron;
+c h2o&olive&pea/
T presrvedlem/s+p.
Cvr‑h@350°F.

DESSERTS

Could there be a lovelier simple pleasure than making and sharing sweet treats? Velvety persimmon pudding, lush coffee-steeped dates with Greek yogurt, a moist carrot cake—this section offers many of my favorite recipes. They express myriad imaginings to the end of an evening of great food: fruit-forward and subtly spiced apricot Platz; dense and decadent chocolate midnight cake; rich but not cloying butterscotch pudding. There's also a range of candies, cupcakes and cookies, such as gooey caramel apples, pleasantly tart lemon cupcakes and crunchy wine biscotti. Once your friends and family taste them, be prepared to share the recipes as well!

CANDIES

THE BEST CARAMEL APPLES are made with small, crisp, sweet-tart fruit; Pink Lady, Granny Smith and Fuji are all suitable varieties.

CARAMEL APPLES

Stir2c sug@med to brwn; slowly+c cream offheat. Put stick in bottom of 8sm unwaxedapple; dip in mix. Cool on waxpaper.

FRUIT & NUT CHOCOLATE

Spread on waxpaper in deep bkgsheet c tstdnut/¼c dried apricot&raisin&citrus&ging. Cvr w 8oz mltdchoc. Chill,shatter.

MINT CREAMS

Beat eggwt stiff; fold +2¾c pdrdsug/5drop mintoil. Spoon by t to waxpaper; chill. Half dip in ½c melteddrkchoc. Chill. Yld~20.

ROSE DELIGHT

Boil5c sug/c h2o>260°F; +mixd 2c strch/t crmoftartar/3c h2o. Simmr h; +2T rosewater. Fill grsdsqpan 8h. Cube7x7,dust w pdrdsug.

COOKIES

SET DOUGH 2" APART ON baking sheet. For soft cookies, remove when a finger tap leaves a slight imprint; for crisp, when it feels just firm.

AMARETTI

Whip2eggwt; fold+mixd
c grndalmond&pdrdsug.
Pipe15 onto parchment;
rest4h uncvrd.
~15m@325°F to brwn.

BISCOTTI

Cream⅓c sug/3T oil/egg;
+ c flr/t bkgpdr/
½t aniseed(opt).
Roll log to fit bkgsheet,
pat squat.
30m@375°F.
Slice14; bake+6m/side.

WINE BISCOTTI

Knead5T sug/⅓c olvoil/
3T wine/¼t soda&bkgpdr
&cardamom/1½c flr.
Roll log to fit bkgsheet,pat
squat. h@325°F.
Slice16; h@225°F.

BOTH CHOCOLATE CHIP CAMPS
are covered here: The first
recipe yields cookies that
are soft with crisp edges, the
second, big and chewy ones.

ROOM TEMPERATURE EGGS
are best for baking; they won't
coagulate butter in cream
mixtures and they beat higher.

Ⓜ CHOCOLATE CHIP COOKIES

Mix¼c buttr&br&wt sug/
T cornsyrup; +egg/t vanil;
+c flr/½t soda/dash salt/
½c chocchip.
Form20balls.
12m@375°F.

Ⓜ CAFÉ-STYLE CHOCOLATE CHIP COOKIES

Cream6T buttr/c brnsug;
+egg/yolk/t vanil; c flour/
¼t soda&salt/½c chocchip.
Form9balls.
18m@325°F.

Ⓥ COCONUT-ALMOND CHIP COOKIES

Add¾c tstdcocont/
½c slicedalmond w
chocchips to dough in either
ChocolateChipCookies.

CHOCOLATE NUT COOKIES

Cream5T buttr&nutbuttr&sug;
+egg/¼t vanil&salt.
Mix+c flr/½t bkgpdr;
+¼c chocchip.
Wrap,chill log.
Cut20.
8m@400°F.

CRUNCH COOKIES

Mix½c buttr&br&wt sug;
+btnegg/T corn syrup; +c flr&
chocchip&trailmix/½t bkgpdr&
salt&cinn/¼t soda.
Form30balls.
8m@375°F.

GINGERBREAD

Mix½c buttr&brsug&molasses/
btnegg/¼c milk.
Knead+2t dryging&cinn/
¼t clove&pep/2c flr.
Chill,roll¼". Cut~10.
10m@350°F.

GINGERSNAPS

Beat½c buttr/c sug; +egg/
¼c molasses/2c flr/
¼c candicdging/2t dryging
&soda/t cinn&clove.
Dip24balls in c sug.
7m@375°F.

LIME MACAROONS

Stir12m@low2eggwt/
½c sug/1¼c cocont/2T flr;
+½t salt/t vanil/2limezest.
Scoop30t to parchment.
10m@300°F.

OATMEAL BISCUITS

Cream⅓c buttr&brsug.
Beat+¼c h2o; +c flr&
quickoals/½t soda/t cinn.
Roll thin,cut~36.
10m@350°F on grsdpan.

FOR BEST RESULTS, SOAK
the raisins below in hot black
tea for an hour, then drain. A
quarter cup of nuts or coconut
may be added as well.

TIP

OATMEAL COOKIES

Cream½c buttr&brsug/⅓c sug;
+egg; +c oat&raisin(opt)/
¾c flr/1½t SweetSpice&vanil/
½t salt&soda.
Form16balls.
10m@350°F.

OLIVE-OIL COOKIES

Beat egg/⅓c olvoil/
⅓c h2o/T lem.
Fold+c flr/⅓c sug/
½t mincdrosemry(opt)/
¼t bkgpdr&s+p.
Form20balls.
12m@375°F.

CINNAMON SABLÉS

Cream½c buttr&sug;
+btnegg/t vanil.
Mix+2c flr/t cinn/½t
bkgpdr&salt/dash cayenne.
Form disc,chill.
Roll,cut18.
12m@350°F.

SHORTBREAD

SCOTLAND Cream
3T fine&pdrd sug/c buttr;
mix+5T riceflr/1½c flr/
t cardamom(opt).
Roll to fit bkgsheet,score24.
h@275°F.
Cut hot.

SNICKERDOODLES

Cream½c buttr&sug;
+btnegg/t vanil; +c flr/
½t nutmeg&salt/¾t bkgpdr.
Mix well.
Roll21balls in 2T sug&cinn.
15m@350°F.

FRUIT DESSERTS

TIP

USE A VARIETY OF EVENLY diced fruits—such as cherries, grapes, pineapple, apricot or pears (peeling is optional)— in the casserole below.

TIP

SOME SUMMER DAYS, you want to make a traditional crumb-topped fruit crisp; on others, a more rustic, less fussy quick crisp is ideal.

FRUIT CASSEROLE

Lyr4c fruit/3T lem/
2c cocont in grsdpan.
Top w ⅓c brsug&grnd
almond/3T liqueur.
Dot w buttr.
25m@300°F.

Ⓜ SLOW PEACH CRISP

Cut c flr/½c buttr&wt&br sug/
t SweetSpice/¼t salt.
Mix4c peach/½lem+zest/
2T maple; top w flrmix.
Cvr15m@350°F;
+35m uncvrd.

Ⓜ QUICK PEACH CRISP

Top8slicedpeach w ¼t cinn&
cardamom&drying&salt/
3T lem; +mixd ½c brsug&
flr&oats/⅓c buttr.
Brwn40m@350°F.

Ⓥ APPLE CRISP

In either PeachCrisp, sub
apples for peaches and
increase wtsug to a cup.

Ⓥ MOLASSES
APPLE CRISP

In either PeachCrisp, decrease
brsug by ½; +dash cloves/
⅓c fancymolasses w topping;
sub apples for peaches.

TIP   TO MAKE A LOVELY
embellishment, pool a little
Maple Cream around each
serving of hot fruit crisp.

MAPLE CREAM

Stir c crm/⅓c maple.
Simmr~15m@med-low to
reduce by ⅓.

COFFEE-STEEPED
DATES

Boil2c strong coffee/t sug/
10cardamom/cinnstick;
+2c pitddate.
Refrigerate>6h.
Srv w greek yogurt.

BANANA RUM FLAMBÉ

Mix¼c mltdbuttr/T lem&zest/
4chopdbanana; top w
¼c brsug.
15m@350°F.
Heat¼c rum; top
fruit,flambé,baste.
Srv w IceCream.

BANANA FRITTERS

Toss4chopdbanana/
2T lem&pdrdsug.
Beat c flr/⅔c h2o/2T oil.
Cvr30m; fold+2whipdeggwt.
Dip,deepfry@325°F.
Srv w IceCream.

KNEDLIKY, STEAMED CZECH
dumplings, should be fat with
fruits such as halved plums
or apricots. Serve with Crème
Fraîche and powdered sugar.

TIP

KNEDLIKY

CZECH Mix T yeast/
c warmmilk/¼c sug&flr.
Knead+2c flr/egg/t salt/
3T oil; rise h.
Roll16; seal over
T PreservedFruit e.
Steam15m.

MY DANISH-CANADIAN FRIEND
Lise provides evidence that
northern cuisine need not be
stodgy: her lemon mousse is
light and vibrantly citrusy.

TIP

LISE'S LEMON MOUSSE

Mix T gelatin/2lem&zest/
¼c hot h2o.
Cream6yolk/c sug; +gelatin.
Beat6eggwt snowy,whip c crm.
Fold lem+wts,crm.
Chill6h.

FIRED PEACHES

Sauté¼c buttr&brsug/
3c peach/dash nutmeg;
+½c rum; flambé,baste.
Scorch,scatter4sprg lavender
on peaches.
Srv w IceCream.

POACHED RHUBARB

Mix lb rhubarb/c SimpleSyrup/
⅓c grenadine.
Heat to 150°F; pour in
heatproof bowl.
Chill6h.

PUDDINGS

A DECADENT HYBRID OF chocolate cake and soufflé, Lava Cake should be eaten straight from the oven so that its interior is still molten.

LAVA CAKE

Mlt⅓c choc&buttr&cocoa; mix+¾c flr&sug/⅓c milk/ 2t vanil&bkgpdr in sqpan. Top(don't mix)+5T cocoa&br& wt sug/1½c coffee. 45m@325°F.

RASPBERRY CRANACHAN

SCOTLAND Whip½c crm/ 2T honey; fold w btn ½c CreamCheese. Lyr2x w 2c berry. Top w 3T tstdsteelcutoats& mixd honey&whisky.

TIP

THE MOMENT YOUR SUGAR has browned, pour into the soufflé dish to prevent burning. Flan is done when a knife comes out clean from the center.

CHOCOLATE MOUSSE

Beat4eggwt.
Gently mlt7oz drkchoc;slowly
+3T buttr&hot h2o&espresso.
Cool slightly; mix+4yolk.
Fold all; chill2h.

PLACING RAMEKINS BRIEFLY in a shallow bath of hot water helps release Panna Cotta. Serve this light dessert wlth berries or Cherry Sauce.

TIP

FLAN

Stir c sug@med to brwn.
Pour in,tilt to coat qt souffledish; +btn can evap& cond milk/5egg/t vanil.
h@350°F in bainmaric.
Chill4h, Invert.

RASPBERRY FOOL

ENGLAND Mix2c raspberry/
T sug&raspberryliqueur(opt).
Whip c crm/~3T sug.
Fold all.
Fill glasses; chill.
Top w berries&mint.

PANNA COTTA

Mix¼c lem/2t gelatin.
Simmr c crm&milk/¼c sug/
½ vanilbeanseeds&pod.
Rmv pod; mix in gelatin.
Fill4grsdramekin/chill>3h.
Invert.

BUTTERSCOTCH PUDDING

Mix½c packedbrsug/3T strch/
¼t salt; +1½c milk/½c crm.
Whisk/boil1m; +2T buttr/
T scotch/t vanil.
Cvr,cool.

BRIOCHE IS A FRENCH BREAD enriched with butter and eggs. It elevates Bread Pudding with Whisky Sauce from a humble dessert to divinity.

THIS FAVORITE IS PART pudding, part cake, redolent with sweet and spicy persimmon, and anticipated each autumn. Serve hot with Ice Cream.

BRIOCHE PUDDING

Mix egg/3T sug/½c milk&crm/
t vanil&cinn; +2c stalebrioche.
Rest20m in buttrdpan;
top w T mltdbuttr&sug.
h@325°F.

WHISKY SAUCE

Mix2T mltdbuttr/¼c sug/egg.
Stir@med-low to boil;
beat+T whisky.
Cool.

STOVETOP RICE PUDDING

Sauté2T buttr/½c arborio/
¼t cardamom&cinn; bring to
boil+2½c milk/2T honey/
lemzest.
Cvr,simmr30m.
Stir occas.

PERSIMMON PUDDING

Mix2c flr/1½c sug/t salt&
cinn&bkgpdr in loafpan;
+2c veryripe persimmon flesh/
2t soda/c milk&nut(opt).
h@350°F.

Ⓜ BAKED RICE PUDDING

Mix3c milk/c cookdrice/
3btnegg/⅓c sug&raisin(opt)/
t vanil/¼t salt&SweetSpice.
Fill buttrddish.
1½h@325°F in bainmarie.

Ⓥ FRUIT & RICE PUDDING

Sub c sm pces fruit(eg
orange,berries,apple,date) for
raisins in BakedRicePudding.
Srv w ClottedCream.

RIS A L'AMANDE IS A CLASSIC
Danish Xmas dish; Rødgrød
med Fløde, packed with
mixed berries and cherries,
a summer one.

RIS A L'AMANDE

DENMARK Boil2c milk/
c arborio.
Cvr45m@low.
Cool; +2T sug/c chopd
almond+1 whl for luck.
Whip2c crm; fold.
Srv w CherrySauce.

CHERRY SAUCE

DENMARK Drain
2c PreservedCherries.
Heat@med+¼c kirsch;
stir+mixd T strch/3T h2o.
Srv on Ris a l'Almande at xmas.

RØDGRØD MED FLØDE

DENMARK Boil3c h2o/c berries
&freshcurrant&cherry/c sug.
Sieve; +mixd ½c strch&h2o.
Stir@med until thick.
Top w whipdcrm.

CHOCOLATE A LA TAZA:

SPAIN Mlt8oz drkchoc/
2c h2o; +2c milk/c h2o
+3T strch&sug.
Stir~7m@med(until thick as
crm); +½t vanil.

FOR THIS UBIQUITOUS
Italian "pick me up," use the
best coffee and rum you can
get your hands on and layer
in a square glass cake pan.

TIRAMISU

Beat yolk/2T sug&rum/
c mascarpone; whip c crm;
fold in.
Mix c espresso/2T rum.
Lyr2x~10ladyfinger/spooned
rum&crm mixes/cocoa.
Chill.

PIES

KEEP PASTRY COLD WHILE making, hot while baking. Use cold fat and ice water, and preheat the oven a bit high, then lower before baking.

LOOK NO FURTHER FOR A traditional go-to dough for double-crusted pies. For best results, add water with a light hand and mix minimally.

PIE DOUGH
Per dbl 9"crust, foodproc
2c flr/t salt/½c buttr&
shortening(or lard)to crumbs.
Sprinkle+2T vinegr/~6T h2o
to ball.
Wrap,chill30m.

SWEET STRUDEL DOUGH
Cut c flr/⅛t salt/
2T btnegg&mltdbuttr.
Knead+4T h2o.
Ball up,cvr~h.
On flrdcloth gently
roll,pull22"sq.
Trim,buttr.

TIP

THIS DOUGH'S WORTH THE extra effort when you want a super-flaky crust (you won't notice the vodka, but you will the crispness it creates).

TIP

THIS EASY, NO-ROLL CRUMB crust is best for no-bake pies, especially pudding-filled ones or Berry Pie, that are served at room temperature.

VODKA PIE DOUGH

Per dbl 9"crust, cut2½c flr/
t salt/2T sug/½c buttr&
shortening(or lard); +c flr.
Sprinkle+¼c h2o&vodka,ball.
Wrap,chill30m.

GRAHAM CRACKER CRUST

Per 9"crust, foodproc
c grahamcracker/2T sug/
5T mltdbuttr.
Spread,pat firmly in pieplate.
Brwn16m@325°F.
Cool.

TIP

A PREBAKED PIE SHELL CAN be made from half of either Pie Dough. It's recommended for wet fillings such as pumpkin because it won't get soggy.

TIP

TO DUST EVENLY WITH cocoa, cinnamon or powdered sugar, spoon into a fine-mesh tea strainer, then tap the strainer lightly with a spoon.

PREBAKED PIE SHELL

Roll½PieDough,place in
bottom of pieplate.
Trim,flute edges.
Brush bottom w eggwt.
Cvr edges w foil.
Bakeblind15m@400°F.

CHERRY CLAFOUTIS

Beat¾c milk/5T flr/2egg/
3T sug/2t vanil;
+¼" in grsdpieplate.
7m@350°F; +45m w
3c cherry/3T sug/batter.
Dust w pdrdsug.

APPLE PIE

Roll2PieDough.
Toss5c apple/¾c sug/
T lem&flr/t SweetSpice;
fill bottomcrust.
Dot w buttr; +top,seal,slit.
10m@400°F; +45m@325°F.

TIP

THIS IS LIGHTER AND FLAKIER
than traditional apple pie.
Use a half batch of Puff Pastry
(recipe in Savory Pies) or a
sheet of store-bought.

BOTTOMLESS
APPLE PIE

Mix5c apple/3T quicktapioca/
½c br&wt sug/t SweetSpice,
fill pieplate.
Top w PuffPastryDough,slit.
30m@425°F; +30m@350°F.

BERRY PIE

Mix6c blue&blk&raspberry.
Puree2c,sieve; +mixd
½c sug/3T strch.
Simmr thick; +T lem.
Fill GrahamCrackerCrust,
top w 4c mixdberry.

CHERRY PIE

Mix2T strch&h2o;
+4c drained Preserved
Cherries/t vanil.
Fill PieShell; +dots buttr/
topcrust/2T sug/slit.
10m@400°F; +35m@325°F.

PUMPKIN PIE

Mix,heat10½oz can pumpkin/
c brsug/2T SweetSpice/
½t salt; +½c crm&milk.
Beat+4btnegg.
Fill PieShell.
25m@400°F(center jiggly).

FRUIT STRUDEL

Coat StrudelDough w
½c grndalmond.
Mix3c fruit/¼c sug.
Pile along dough edge.
Fold up,buttr.
30m@350°F(buttr1x).

THIS MARVELOUS TART
was shared with me by
@margiememo. It's from
her friend Augusta, who is
in her 80s and claims the
recipe is foolproof.

TIP

AUGUSTA'S BLUEBERRY TART

Cut½c buttr/c flr/2T sug/
¼t salt; +T vinegr.
Press in pieplate,
+3c berry/½c sug/2T flr.
45m@400°F.
Top w 2c berry.

BUTTER TARTS ARE UNIQUE
to Canada. Golden treacle,
imported from Britain, is a
beet sugar syrup; golden corn
syrup may be used instead.

TIP

BUTTER TARTS

CANADA Roll,cut PieDough
to fit 6muffincup.
Bakeblind3m@375°F;
+20m filld w btnegg/c brsug/
2T crm&treacle/1½t vinegr&
vanil.

FROSTINGS

TIP

EACH OF THESE ELEGANT, OLD-fashioned recipes will frost a double-layer cake; make a half-batch to frost 12 cupcakes.

SHEILA LUKINS'S CREAM CHEESE FROSTING

Cream c CreamCheese/ ⅔c buttr; sift,beat in 3c pdrd sug; +t vanil/¼c lem(opt).

GINGER CREAM CHEESE FROSTING

Cream c CreamCheese/4T buttr/ 2t ging/⅛t salt&vanil; sift in,beat+3c pdrdsug.

EGG YOLKS GIVE THESE Buttercreams a notably airy, velvety texture. Without them, they will be more plainly buttery, but still delicious.

THE BUTTERCREAMS WILL keep up to 5 days without the raw yolks. Omit them when serving the elderly, immuno-compromised, or small children.

TIPS

Ⓜ JULIA CHILD'S BUTTERCREAM ICING

Cream c buttr/4yolk(opt)/T vanil; sift in+1⅓c pdrdsug. Beat5m@med; chill slightly. Chill iced cake; eat<d.

Ⓥ FLAVORED BUTTERCREAM ICING

Sub t flavored extract (almond/coconut/kirsch/lem/maple/mint/rum/etc) for vanil.

Ⓥ LAVENDER BUTTERCREAM ICING

Grnd to pdr t dry english lavender/T sug; +to pdrdsug.

Ⓥ LIQUOR BUTTERCREAM ICING

Sub3T of spirits (brandy/irishcream/kirsch/mint/orange/rum/whisky/etc) for vanil.

Ⓥ CHOCOLATE BUTTERCREAM ICING

Sub2oz mltdchoc for vanil; +T cocoa w pdrdsug.

Ⓥ COFFEE BUTTERCREAM ICING

Slowly+2T coffee (strongcoffee/espresso) in place of vanil.

Ⓥ CITRUS BUTTERCREAM ICING

Slowly+½t lem or lime or orange zest/3T lem or lime or oj/dash salt w pdrdsug.

AS WONDERFUL AS CHOCOLATE Buttercream is, I often prefer this smoother, glossier icing, which accentuates dark chocolate's bittersweetness.

TIP

DECEPTIVELY SWEET CHOCOLATE ICING

Gently mlt6oz drkchoc; gradually mix in ½c srcrm. Chill slightly.

CAKES

TIPS

GIVE THE BAKING PANS (EVEN NONSTICK ONES) A LIGHT, EVEN buttering and flouring when making any of these cakes so they'll slip out easily.

ANGEL FOOD CAKE IS BEST MADE IN A TALL, UNGREASED TUBE pan. Bundt pans won't easily release the cake. Serve with berries and whipped cream.

ANGEL FOOD CAKE

Beat11eggwt foamy.
Beat snowy+1½t crmoftartar.
Beat stiff+1½c sug.
Fold+c flr/t vanil. Fill tubepan.
h@325°F.
Cool well.

CHOCOLATE DECADENCE CAKE

Mlt2c choc/⅔c buttr;
beat+⅔c coffee&flr&cocoa.
Cream c sug/3egg.
Fold all; fill sqpan.
40m@350°F in bainmarie.

IN THE TRADITION OF Scandinavian immigrants to northern Canada, where I'm from, lovely unfrosted cakes are eaten with coffee or ice cream.

APPLE CAKE

CANADA Cream½c buttr/c sug.
Mix+2egg/⅔c milk; 2c flr/
2t soda/½t salt/t cinn&
nutmeg.
Fold+4c apple; fill cakepan.
40m@325°F.

CRUMB CAKE

Rub c sug/¾c buttr/
2c flr to crumbs; rsv c.
Mix rest/c buttrmilk/
t soda&cinn&clove/egg.
Fill cakepan, top w c crumbs.
45m@350°F.

A PLATZ IS EQUAL PARTS coffee cake and crisp. An amazing transformation occurs in fruits baked this way: They become rich, jammy and tart.

Ⓜ APRICOT PLATZ

MENNONITE Mix½c milk&sug/
c flr/t bkgpdr&vanil/
5T mltdbuttr/btnegg.
Fill sqpan; top+9halved
apricot/⅓c buttr&flr&sug.
h@350°F.

Ⓥ SOUR CHERRY PLATZ

Sub2c srcherry for apricots
& kirsch for vanil.

Ⓥ RHUBARB PLATZ

Sub3c dicedrhubarb tossed w
c sug for apricots.

CELEBRATE GREAT OCCASIONS and great people by baking the following double-layer cakes lavished with your choice of frosting.

PARSNIPS LEND A SOPHISTI-cated sweet, nutty flavor to this cake. With Ginger or Cream Cheese Frosting, it's an extraordinary end to a meal.

MIDNIGHT CAKE

Mix3egg/2c sug/c oil&cocoa&
milk/2T triplesec&lem&zest;
+4c flr/2t bkgpdr/
t salt&soda&cinn.
Fill2cakepan.
30m@350°F.

NUT CAKE

Mix2c flr/2T cinn/
c finely chopdnut/T bkgpdr.
Cream c buttr/2c sug;
mix+4yolk/c milk.
Fold+4whipdeggwt.
Fill2cakepan.
30m@325°F.

PARSNIP CAKE

Mix2c flr/c sug/2T Sweet
Spice/2t bkgpdr/t salt
 w mixd⅔c oil&milk/4egg/
2t vanil; +2c grtdparsnip.
Fill2cakepan.
25-30m@350°F.

VANILLA CAKE

Cream¾c buttr/1½c sug.
Alternately beat+c milk/
T vanil/2c cakeflr/T bkgpdr/
t salt. Fold+5whipdeggwt.
Fill2cakepan.
18m@350°F.

THIS EXCEPTIONALLY FLUFFY Carrot Cake should be frosted with Sheila Lukins's Cream Cheese Frosting.

TO MAKE PUREED CARROTS, cover and simmer a pound peeled, chopped carrots in a cup of water 15 minutes, then blend to a smooth consistency.

SHEILA LUKINS'S CARROT CAKE

Beat3c flr&sug/T soda&cinn& vanil/t salt/4egg/1½c oil.
Fold+1½c cocont&walnt& carrotpuree.
Fill2cakepan.
50m@350°F.

CUPCAKES

IT'S BEST TO BAKE CUPCAKES A FEW HOURS AHEAD SO THAT they can cool and firm completely. Then top with the icing of your choice.

DEEPEN THE FLAVOR OF DESSERTS CONTAINING CHOCOLATE, spices and coffee by adding a little instant espresso powder, sold at Italian grocers.

THESE TWO CHOCOLATE CUPCAKES ARE QUITE DIFFERENT. THE first is mildly chocolaty, like hot cocoa, while the second is more dark and intense.

CHOCOLATE CUPCAKES

Cream8T buttr/c sug;
+2btnegg. Sift¼t soda&
salt&SweetSpice/c flr/
½c cocoa/½t bkgpdr.
Mix all+½c milk.
Fill12.
20m@375°F.

DEVIL'S CUPCAKES

Cream c buttr/2c sug/2egg;
+4oz mltdchoc/2T lem/
⅔c cocoa&espresso&crm;
+2c flr/t soda/½t bkgpdr&salt.
Fill12.
20m@350°F.

LEMON CUPCAKES

Cream6T buttr/⅔c sug.
Beat+2egg/2T lem&zest/
½c yogurt; fold+1⅓c flr/
½t bkgpdr&soda.
Fill12.
20m@350°F.

TIP

DON'T FROST THE RHUBARB
Cupcakes—they form their
own rustic topping. Turn
upside-down after cooling
briefly and loosening with
a knife.

RHUBARB UPSIDE-DOWN CUPCAKES

Cream½c sug&mltdbuttr/
2egg/c yogurt,+2c flr/
2t bkgpdr/t sall.
Buttr,flll12;+3T sug&rhubarb/
batter e.
25m@350°F.

ICE CREAMS & SORBETS

TIPS

MAKING ICE CREAM WITHOUT A MACHINE REQUIRES ABUNDANT hours near the freezer. Make a day ahead and whisk every hour until no puddling occurs.

THIS CUSTARD-BASED HONEY ICE CREAM IS THE FOUNDATION for several other flavors. The vodka prevents ice crystals, but may be omitted.

Ⓜ HONEY ICE CREAM

Stir6yolk/2c milk/
½c sug&honey/¼t salt
in bainmarie until thick.
Chill; +2c crm/T vodka.
Freeze5h(mix1x/h) or use
machine.

Ⓥ DARK CHOCOLATE ICE CREAM

Mix2T cocoa/dash
cayenne(opt) w sug in
HoneyIceCream; +6oz
grtdchoc w milk.

Ⓥ CHOCOLATE MINT ICE CREAM

Heat3c mint w milk in
HoneyIceCream.
Strain; +6oz grtdchoc
when~½frozen.

Ⓥ COFFEE ICE CREAM

Heat2c coffeebean w milk in
HoneyIceCream; cvr,steep>h
or to taste.
Strain.

Ⓥ STRAWBERRY ICE CREAM

Reduce sug in HoneyIceCream
by ¼c. Mash2c strawberry/
T lem&vanil/¼c sug; stir into
milk.

Ⓥ VANILLA ICE CREAM

Add seeds of split vanilbean
to milk in HoneyIceCream
(or T vanilextract to crm).

Ⓥ WHISKY ICE CREAM

Beat5T scotch or bourbon well
w crm in HoneyIceCream.

BASIL ICE CREAM

Blend can evap&cond milk/
c crm/3yolk/mincd bnch
basil/½t salt/2T olvoil.
Chill. Freeze5h(mix1x/h)
or use machine.

STOUT ICE CREAM

Boil,cool⅔c stout/
2T fancymolasses.
Beat4yolk/⅓c sug;
+c milk&crm/stoutmix.
Chill. Freeze5h(mix1x/h)
or use machine.

MANGO SORBET

Dissolve2t gelatin/
2T hot h2o; mix+¼c lem/
2c mangopuree/T rum.
Chill,beat; fold+whipdeggwt.
Freeze5h(mix1x/h)
or use machine.

WINE SORBET

Simmr3c roséwine/½c sug to
reduce to c; +¼c honey/T lem.
Chill. Freeze5h(mix1x/h)
or use machine.

DRINKS

Meals provide food, but a banquet is splendid with drink. Beverages offer easy ways to delight in new flavors, to add nuance to menus, and to balance the palates of your guests. To get to the heart of the matter, read up on pairing wine and food in creative ways, based on flavor and aroma profiles of each grape varietal, rather than by any old-fashioned hard-and-fast rules. To quench everyday thirsts to particular satisfaction, bottle up your own glowing homemade syrups to mix into sodas, hot drinks, and to drizzle on desserts. Warm special occasions with mulled cider in wintertime, and chill out with @poormojo's sangria on long summer nights. Or brew up some slower elixirs, from root beer to limoncello, to really spice up your home bartending. On that note, cocktails are fun, too. If measuring jiggers gives you a headache before you've even had a sip, I think you'll be delighted by these tiny recipes, doled out by measuring cup and spoon. Each makes one drink. *Santé!*

SYRUPS

TIP

SIMPLE SYRUPS ADD DEPTH to desserts, drinks and fruit salads and make good gifts. If you'd like to can them, fill clean jars and boil 10m.

BERRY SYRUP

Simmr2c mixd or single berry/T lem&h2o@low~5m; sieve.
Mix+can frozen juice; boil2m.
Refrigerate.
Yld~3c.

CHOCOLATE SYRUP

Sift1½ c sug/c cocoa; slowly whisk in c h2o.
Simmr/stir3m; +2t vanil.
Refrigerate.
Yld1¾c.

GINGER SYRUP

Dice½lb ging; +4c h2o/ c brsug/cinnstick/dash cayenne.
Simmr~40m,sieve.
Refrigerate.
Yld~2c.

HONEY SYRUP

Simmr¾c honey/¼c h2o/
2T lem/¼t lemzest to
reduce by ¼.
Refrigerate.
Yld c.

SIMPLE SYRUP

Stir2c sug&h2o@med to
dissolve; bring to boil.
Yld2c.

VANILLA SYRUP

Scrape½vanilbean in c h2o/
2c sug; +pod.
Stir@med to dissolve.
Refrigerate.
Yld2c.

THESE ARE COCKTAIL STAPLES:
Falernum is the tropical in rum
drinks; Grenadine, the glow to
Singapore Slings; Orgeat, the
key to Mai Tais.

FALERNUM SYRUP

Tst whl T allspice/t clove/
nutmeg; +½c limezest&ging/
c rum; soak24h.
Mix+c SimpleSyrup/
¼t almondextract.
Refrigerate.
Yld2c.

GRENADINE SYRUP

Seed,boil2lb pomegranate/
c h2o to burst; strain
(or buy juice).
Mix+equal volume sug;
boil,dissolve.
Refrigerate.
Yld~c.

ORGEAT SYRUP

Boil3½c h2o/c chopdalmond/
c sug; soak12h.
Strain in muslin; +3c sug.
Stir@med to dissolve/boil.
Refrigerate.
Yld2c.

ELIXIRS

MULLED CIDER

Heat@low>3h 6c softapple
cider/cinnstick&staranise/
5clove&pepcorn&cardamom/
½vanilbean/c orange/
t zest&ging.
Srv4 w brandy(opt).

EGGNOG

Shake hard 1¼c rum/
½c SimpleSyrup/⅓c crm/
2c milk/4dash bitters/
½t freshly grtdnutmeg/4egg.
Top w nutmeg&cinn.
Srv4.

LIMONCELLO

ITALY Mix12lemzest/
btl 100proofvodka; cvr2wk.
Strain; +2nd 750ml vodka/
2c boiled,cooled sug&h2o.
Bottle>4wk.
Srv cold.
Yld8c.

MELON FIZZ

Blend c ice/⅓c elderflower
syrup/3T lem/3c melon.
Srv promptly topped w
clubsoda/mint in cold glasses.
Srv w vodka(opt).
Srv4.

TIP

REAL ROOT BEER IS A
revelation. Health-food stores
stock sassafras. Use 4-8 oz
jars as testers; chill bailtops
as soon as the soda's fizzy.

ROOT BEER

Boil,cool,strain16c h2o/
vanilbean/⅔c sassafras/
3T wintergreen/3c brsug;
+⅛t aleyeast.
Fill6x pt bailtop+4 testers.
Test fizz 2-7d.

SPICED RUM

TRINIDAD Mix, seal in jar
btl drkrum/orangezest/
smashedwhlnutmeg/
3cinnstick/ 2staranise/
t whlallspice.
Infuse>2wk.
Yld25oz.

SPICED MILK TEA

THAILAND Per srvg, boil c h2o/
cinnstick&staranise&clove;
+2bag blktea/T brsug 5m.
Strain tea,chill.
Srv on ice; top w crm.

TIP

THIS SANGRIA IS THE NECTAR
of espionage, involving
@poormojo's mom, a favorite
restaurant's secret recipe, and
a revealing bin of empties.

@POORMOJO'S SANGRIA

Mix,chill btl Lambrusco
rdwine/6T oj&pineapjuice/
¼c triplesec&gingbrandy&
vodka&papayajuice/
2T amaretto&lime.
Srv4.

COCKTAILS

BRANDY ALEXANDER

Shake hard w ice 3T brandy/
2T crèmedecacao&crm.
Strain into cocktail glass.
Dust w pinch nutmeg.

TIP

TO SIMPLIFY MAKING FIERY
cocktails, briefly warm the
liquor in a small covered
saucepan so you can bring it
closer to the ignition point.

COMBUSTIBLE EDISON

Shake2T campari&lem/ice;
strain into cold cocktail glass.
Warm¼c brandy; ignite,pour
in flaming stream into glass.

COSMOPOLITAN

Shake w ice ¼c vodka&
cointreau&cranberryjuice/
2T lime cordial&juice/
2dash orangebitters.
Strain into cocktail glass.

DARK & STORMY

Lyr in ice-filled tumbler
⅔c drkrum/2T FalernumSyrup/
¼c lime/dash aromaticbitters/
gingbeer to fill.

FOG CUTTER

Shake w ice ¼c goldrum/
2T brandy&lem&oj/
T gin&OrgeatSyrup.
Strain to highball of ice.
Float w dry sherry.

GIN & TONIC

Lyr in highball of ice
3T gin/tonic to fill.
Float w T gin.
Garnish w slice
lime&cuke(opt).

HOT BUTTERED RUM

Lyr in warm toddymug
¼c goldrum/t buttr.
Fill w hot h2o; +brsug
to taste.
Garnish w cinnstick.

HOT TODDY

Lyr in warm toddymug
lemslice studded w 4clove/
¼c whisky/1½T SImpleSyrup/
hot h2o to fill.

MAI TAI

Shake w ice 2T wtrum/
T orangecuraçao&OrgeatSyrup/
2t lime/t SImpleSyrup;
strain to highball of ice.
Float w 2T drkrum;
+limeslice.

MINT JULEP

Muddle in highball 5sprg
spearmint/⅓c bourbon/
2T cold h2o/¼c SImpleSyrup;
fill,churn w crushedice.
Top w crushedice&mint.

MOJITO

Muddle¼c goldrum&lime/
2T SimpleSyrup/5sprg mint/
2dash aromaticbitters.
Shake w ice; strain to
highball of ice.
Float w T rum.

TIP

IN TRINIDAD, PITCHERS OF
this Rum de Crème milk
cooler, similar to eggnog, are
enjoyed on special occasions.

RUM DE CRÈME

TRINIDAD Blend2c SpicedRum
&irishcrm/c milk&condmilk/
T cinn/freshly grtdnutmeg/
2 egg/3dash bitters.
Srv on ice.

RUM EGGNOG

Shake hard w ice
⅓c goldrum&milk/
2T SimpleSyrup/2t crm/
egg/dash aromaticbitters
into highball.
Dust w SweetSpice.

SAZERAC

Stir w ice ¼c ryewhisky&
brandy/3dash aromaticbitters/
t SimpleSyrup; strain to short
glass rinsed w t absinthe.

SINGAPORE SLING

Shake ice/¼c gin/
½c pineapjuice/3T lem/
2T cherrybrandy/T Grenadine/
1½t cointreau&bénédictine/
bitters.
Strain; top w cherry.

WINE & FOOD PAIRING SUGGESTIONS

T he old rule "red with meat, white with fish" isn't as helpful now that ethnic and fusion dishes are so commonplace. Use these more comprehensive notes as a guide.

— WHITES —

SERVE WHITE WINES COOL, NOT COLD. TO COOL QUICKLY, bury in ice and salt.

CHARDONNAY Opulent apple/tropical fruit, butter/oak.
Pair w full flavors Creamy, grilled, caramelized seafood/poultry/ meat, cheese.

CHENIN BLANC Pure peach, flowers, minerals.
Pair w spicy-warm food Full, mellow veg/seafood/poultry with clove/ cinnamon, rich cheese.

GEWÜRZTRAMINER Fragrant lychee/tangerine, rose/spice.
Pair w spicy-hot food Richly seasoned, bold Asian poultry/pork, curries/chilies.

GRUNER VELTLINER Fresh lemon/grapefruit, green peas.
Pair w bright flavors Raw, herbal veg/superb seafood, garlic/greens, salad/fruit.

PINOT GRIS (GRIGIO) Lithe stone, melon/kiwi, zest.
Pair w understated flavors Stewed, piquant veg/seafood/poultry/veal. Avoid tomato.

RIESLING Fruity Citrus/peach, flowers.
Pair w mellow flavors Smoky, salty, clean seafood/poultry, fresh herbs, crisp fruit. Avoid sweets.

SAUVIGNON (FUMÉ) BLANC Crisp grass, herbs, citrus.
Pair w light seasonings Delicate, toasted, creamy, lemony veg/seafood, cheese/fruit.

SÉMILLON Earthy grass, figs, nuts, flowers.
Pair w savory-spicy food Herbal, spiced flavors, especially veg/seafood, thyme/cumin.

SPARKLING Euphoric yeast/toast, vanilla/cream, apple/pear.
Pair w nakedly flavorful food Plain seafood, cheese/fruit, hors d'oeuvres.

VIOGNIER Scented apricot/hawthorn, rosehip/flowers, wood.
Pair w fragrant food Sweet, fruity, spicy, Asian seafood/poultry/light meat.

REDS

TIPS **SERVE RED WINES AT ROOM TEMPERATURE, OR COOL** humbler vintages just slightly.

BARBERA Rich low tannins, red fruit/smoke.
Pair w hearty fare Roasted or stewed meats, poultry, pastas.

CABERNET FRANC Savory-med tannins, raspberry/currant, herbal.
Pair w understated flavors Meats/poultry/veg, mild herbal seasonings.

CABERNET SAUVIGNON Refined high tannins, black currants, flowers, minerals.
Pair w complex food Hearty roasted/grilled meat, fatty dishes.

CARMÉNÈRE Herbal med tannins, fruit/cherry, pepper/earth, gamey.
Pair w herbal food Light meats/veg, mellow seasonings.

CORVINA Nutty low tannins, sour cherry/dry fruit, almond/earth.
Pair w direct flavors Fatty meats/sausage/veg, spicy Italian
seasonings.

GAMAY Refreshing minimun tannins, red berries, flowers, earth.
Pair w typical white-matches Lightest meats/poultry/veg, hors
d'oeuvres.

GRENACHE Jammy low tannins, ripe berries/plum, flowers/spice.
Pair w mellow flavors Ground meats/poultry/veg, herbal homey
seasonings.

MALBEC Rustic high tannins, plum/berries, earth/tea.
Pair w robust flavors Hearty roasted/grilled red meats, rich
Provençal seasonings.

MERLOT Lush med tannins, plum/cherry, flowers.
Pair w savory flavors Stewed meats/poultry/veg, tomato, umame,
Mediterranean seasonings.

MONTEPULCIANO Earthy low-med tannins, strawberry/plum,
flowers.
Pair with hearty fare Savory meats/poultry, pasta, Italian seasonings.

NEBBIOLO (BAROLO/BARBARESCO) Weighty maximum tannins,
plum/fig, tar/rose.
Pair w rich food Heartiest red meats, fatty umame seasonings.

PINOT NOIR Delicate low-med tannins, cherry/strawberry, earth.
Pair w soft flavors Light meats/poultry/veg, cheese, subtle seasonings.

SANGIOVESE Aromatic low tannins, plum/cherry, earth/tobacco.
Pair w bright flavors Stewed or roasted meats, pastas, Italian seasonings.

SYRAH (SHIRAZ) Meaty med-high tannins, blackberry/leather, spice.
Pair w big flavors Grilled meats/poultry, rich seasonings.

TEMPRANILLO Velvety low-med tannins, red berries, leather/spices.
Pair w moderate flavors Grilled meats/veg, light spicy seasonings.

ZINFANDEL juicy med tannins, cherry/berries, spice.
Pair w picante food Grilled meats/poultry/veg, tomato/chilies, spicy zesty seasonings.

DESSERT WINES (PORT/SHERRY, SAUTERNES/TOKAJ, ICEWINE) can be white or red. Serve cool. Pair w mild desserts: fruit/cookies, not toffee/cake.

GLOSSARY

TERM	TRANSLATION	MEANING
~	about	approximately; some variation is expected in this step, so use some judgment
+	add	add the next ingredients; also in "s+p," salt and pepper
&	and	in the same amount and in the same step; equal measures of ingredients in a step, e.g. "T flr&sug" means: 1 tablespoon each of flour and sugar; before s+p means T each
/	and	different measures of ingredients in a step; eg mix c flr/T sug means: mix 1 cup of flour and 1 tablespoon of sugar
@	at	indicated temperature, e.g. bake or cook @400°, or designates a Twitter user name
<	less than	"boil<5m" means: boil for up to 5 minutes
>	more than	"boil>5m" means: boil for at least 5 minutes

TERM	TRANSLATION	MEANING
;	next	separates steps, e.g. "boil3m; drain" means: boil for 3 minutes; next drain
,	then	groups actions in a step; e.g. "wash,chop spinach" means wash, then chop the spinach
aspargus	asparagus	
bainmarie	bain-marie	larger baking dish, half full of hot water, in which dishes of delicate food may bake gently
bakeblind	bake blind	bake blind or blind bake; to pre-bake pastry, lined with foil and filled with dry beans or pastry weights, improving final texture
balsamic	balsamic vinegar	sweet oaked vinegar from Italy; invest in aged or gently simmer cheap vinegar until reduced by half
bay	bay leaf	1 dried leaf; remove before serving or pureeing a dish
beat	beat	to mix vigorously until well combined, such as beating eggs
bellpep	bell pepper	green, unless otherwise specified
bkg	baking	
bkgdish	baking dish	aka casserole dish; standard 9"x13", unless otherwise specified

TERM	TRANSLATION	MEANING
bkgpdr	baking powder	pre-mixed baking soda and acid; "double acting" means it reacts to both moisture and heat
bkgsheet	baking sheet	aka cookie sheet, standard 15"x 12"; invest in heavier, insulated sheets to avoid burnt bottoms
blanch(d)	blanch(ed)	to immerse for a short time in boiling water, then ice water
blk	black	
bnch	bunch	standard grocery-store sized; about 1 oz/28g herbs and 1lb/.5kg of leafy greens
bqtgarni	bouquet garni	a tied bundle of fresh and/or dry herbs that is removed before serving
br	brown	the color
brdcrumbs	bread crumbs	unseasoned fine; fresh is best
brnsug	brown sugar	gently packed; dark or light as preferred
broil(d)	broil(ed)	to cook quickly a few inches below a direct heat source
brwn(d)	brown(ed)	to cook over medium-high heat until evenly brown; best to use a heavy pan and a fat with a high smoke point

TERM	TRANSLATION	MEANING
btl	bottle	standard 750 ml bottle for wine and other alcohols, unless otherwise specified
btn	beaten	add the ingredient pre-beaten, e.g. "+btn egg" means add 1 beaten egg
buttr(d)	butter(ed)	unsalted for baking and sweets, salted for everything else
c	cup	8 fluid ounces; solids are diced or sliced as you like, unless otherwise specified
cakepan	cake pan	standard 8" round baking pan, buttered and floured; nonstick is helpful
can(d)	can(ned)	the typical grocery-store option, such as a 10½-ounce can of tomatoes
cherry	cherry	pitted, unless otherwise specified
chili	chili pepper	fresh, seeded, and as hot as desired, unless specified
chilipaste	Thai chili paste	use red chili paste in all recipes
chipotle	canned chipotle pepper in adobo sauce	with sauce where indicated; soaked may be substituted
choc	chocolate	bittersweet, unless otherwise indicated

TERM	TRANSLATION	MEANING
chocchip	chocolate chips	bittersweet or milk chocolate, as preferred
chop(d)	chop(ped)	cut into roughly inch-sized pieces
cinn	cinnamon	ground, unless specified
clove	clove	the spice; ground unless otherwise specified
clv	clove	refers to garlic, whole, peeled, unless otherwise specified
cocont	coconut	unsweetened fine shredded; in the case of milk, "can cocont" means about 10 ounces
cond	condensed	
cont	continue	proceed to the next step
cook(d)	cook(ed)	ingredient is pre-cooked using a standard method, e.g. steamed rice
coriander	coriander	the dried seed of the cilantro herb; ground unless otherwise specified
cornmeal	yellow cornmeal	fine-grain, unless otherwise specified; not corn flour
cream	cream	beat vigorously until a light and pale mixture forms, such as butter and sugar prepared for cookies

TERM	TRANSLATION	MEANING
crm	dairy cream	heavy, unless otherwise specified
cuke	cucumber	medium slicing, unless specified
currant	currants	dry, unless otherwise specified
cut	cut together	to blend dry ingredients and fat into a crumb mixture using a food processor, butter knives, or a pastry cutter
cvr(d)	cover(ed)	cover completely unless specified
dbl	double	
d	day	
deepfry	deep fry	to cook submerged in 350° to 375°F vegetable oil, unless otherwise noted
deglaze	deglaze	to dissolve the caramelized residue from a hot skillet by adding liquid, such as stock or wine, and scraping and stirring
dice	dice(d)	cut into roughly half-inch cubes, or quarter-inch for finely diced
dijon	Dijon-style mustard	a particularly strong mustard; any assertive mustard may be used
driedtom	dried tomatoes	hot-water soaked homemade or store-bought; don't soak oil-packed
drk	dark	

TERM	TRANSLATION	MEANING
e	each	
egg	egg	large, unless otherwise specified
evap	evaporated	
flr	flour	all-purpose white, unless otherwise specified; coated with flour; also as in "cauliflr"
fold	fold together	to combine light and dense mixtures without deflating; gently turn together using a large bowl and wide spatula
foodproc	food processor	use to blend to uniform consistency, unless otherwise specified; also makes quick work of fine chopping and grinding
fruit	fruit	except with lemons and limes, when a fruit such as "pineapple" is listed, use the flesh unless othewise indicated
fry	pan fry	to cook quickly in a small amount of oil or fat
garlc	garlic	one medium-sized clove, minced or pressed, unless otherwise specified
ging	ginger root	fresh, peeled and minced unless otherwise specified
gr	green	such as green bean

TERM	TRANSLATION	MEANING
grnd	grind	to grind to a uniform texture with a food processor or mortar and pestle
grsd	greased	coated lightly with vegetable oil, unless otherwise specified
grt(d)	grate(d)	
h	hour	
h2o	water	at room temperature, unless otherwise noted
hlvd	halved	
herbs	herbs	one or more in the mix and fresh, unless otherwise specified; substitute 1 teaspoon dry per 1 tablespoon fresh
hvy	heavy	such as heavy cream
immed	immediately	this step should be performed promptly
inc	includ(e/ing)	
juliene	julienne	to slice into strips measuring about $\frac{1}{8}$" x $2\frac{1}{2}$"
lem	lemon	juice, unless otherwise specified; buy unwaxed fruit when zest is called for
lgt	light	such as light cream

TERM	TRANSLATION	MEANING
lime	lime	juice, unless otherwise specified; buy unwaxed fruit when zest is called for
loafpan	loaf pan	standard 9" x 5"; be aware that glass bakes hotter than tin or ceramic
lrg	large	
lyr	layer	
m	minute	
maple	maple syrup	grade B, unless otherwise specified
marinate	marinate	to immerse foods in a seasoned, often acidic, liquid before cooking to tenderize and flavor
mash(d)	mashed	crushed quite smooth, such as mashed potatoes
mayo	mayonnaise	homemade is preferable
med	medium	
milk	milk	whole, unless otherwise specified
minc(d)	mince(d)	cut as finely as possible
miso	miso paste	brown or white miso paste, as indicated
mix(d)	mix(ed)	ingredients are mixed well before adding to the recipe
mlt(d)	melt(ed)	

TERM	TRANSLATION	MEANING
mozz	mozzarella	fresh, unless otherwise specified
M	master recipe	denotes recipe on which others are built
muslin	muslin	cheesecloth works fine, too
nec	necessary	variation expected, so use your judgment
nuts	nuts	whole, unless otherwise specified
oats	oats	old-fashioned rolled oats, unless otherwise noted; "quickoats" means quick-cooking
occas	occasionally	
offheat	away from heat	remove item from oven or electric burner, or simply shut off gas burner
oil	oil	any neutral-flavored vegetable oil, such as canola or sunflower
oj	orange juice	try to use fresh-squeezed if the ingredient is key to the dish
olv(oil)	olive(oil)	good tasting olives, pitted, unless otherwise noted; for olive oil, use extra-virgin
onion	onion	one medium-sized, yellow, and diced, unless otherwise specified
opt	optional	may be omitted

TERM	TRANSLATION	MEANING
oreg	oregano	
paprka	paprika	unless otherwise specified, use a basic sweet Hungarian paprika, or if you prefer a smoky flavor, a Spanish one
parm	Parmigiano-Reggiano	hard, dry, nutty Italian cheese used grated, unless otherwise specified; substitute other hard cheese if you like
parsly	parsley	either curly or flat-leaf is fine
pastini	pastini	tiny solid pasta shapes, such as orzo, stars, or alphabets
pce(s)	piece(s)	of average size for the ingredient, unless otherwise specfied
pdr	powder(ed)	such as chili powder or powdered sugar
peas	green peas	fresh or frozen may be used, unless otherwise specified
pectin	packaged pectin	one 2-oz envelope powdered, two 2.8-oz pouches liquid, or one 8-oz bottle liquid
peeld	peeled	
pep	pepper	dry spice; freshly ground black, unless otherwise specified

TERM	TRANSLATION	MEANING
pieplate	pie plate	standard 9" round, medium depth; note that glass bakes hotter than tin or ceramic
pineapjuice	pineapple juice	
pitd	pitted	
pkg	package	standard-sized grocery-store product, such as a 3.4-oz box of instant pudding
pref	preferably	
prick	prick with a fork	perforate the food deeply at even 1" intervals
procsr	food processor	
pt	pint	
qt	quart	
ramekin	ramekin	use ovenproof 3"-wide ramekin or custard cup, unless otherwise noted
rd	red	
rd birdchili	red bird's eye chili	small hot chilies common to South Asian cuisine; seed as desired
rdpcp	crushed red pepper	aka chili flakes

TERM	TRANSLATION	MEANING
rem	remaining	
rmv	remove	
roma	roma tomato	aka plum tomato
rosemry	rosemary	fresh; 1 medium sprig, unless otherwise specified
rpt	repeat	repeat the last step
rsv(d)	reserve(d)	to put aside for later use; also refers to something that was put aside earlier, as in "whisk in rsvd stock"
s+p	salt & pepper	measured to taste, unless specified; if s+p follows "&," as in "3T oil&s+p," use 3T salt and 3T pepper
sauté	sauté	to add fat, then ingredients, to a hot pan, and stir-fry
scalion	scallion	aka green onion; use the white to light-green part, not the drier dark-green part
sesoil	sesame oil	toasted sesame oil is best
sesseed	sesame seeds	white untoasted
sherry	dry cooking sherry	or substitute white wine

TERM	TRANSLATION	MEANING
shroom	mushrooms	white or brown button mushrooms, sliced, unless otherwise specified
sieve	sieve	to strain and/or press through a fine-mesh sieve, or use a food mill, if handy
simmr	simmer	to bring to a boil and continue to boil gently at a lower temperature; partly cover pan, if not otherwise specified
sm	small	
soda	baking soda	sodium bicarbonate needs acid and moisture to react; mix with wet ingredients just before baking
soya	soy sauce	
spaghetti	spaghetti	dry spaghetti; halve cooking time if using fresh
spices	spices	dry ground, unless otherwise specified
sprg	sprig	about 4" of stem, trimmed if necessary, and leaves
sqpan	square pan	standard 9" x 9" baking pan, buttered and floured; nonstick is helpful
sr	sour	such as sour cream
srv(g)	serv(e/ing)	

TERM	TRANSLATION	MEANING
steam(d)	steam(ed)	cooked in a covered steamer until just tender, unless otherwise specified; boil water before adding food
stirfry	stir-fry	to sauté quickly on very high heat, retaining texture and flavor
stock	hot stock	chicken or vegetable "scrap" stock unless specified; homemade is best, but liquids and pastes are better than dried forms
strch	starch	cornstarch, unless otherwise indicated
sub	substitute	
sug	sugar	white, unless specified
t	teaspoon	solids are minced, unless otherwise noted
T	tablespoon	solids are minced, unless otherwise noted
tarrgn	tarragon	
tater	potato	use a medium-sized waxy variety, such as Yukon Gold, unless otherwise noted
tom	tomato	use medium-sized tomatoes; out of season, canned is generally better; use ½ cup chopped canned tomatoes per single fresh

TERM	TRANSLATION	MEANING
tompaste	tomato paste	tubes, which contain highly concentrated paste, are conveniently resealable
tst(d)	toast(ed)	as for nuts, stirred constantly in a dry skillet over medium heat, or a slice of bread
uncvr(d)	uncover(ed)	
V	variation	variation on a master recipe
vanil	vanilla	pure liquid extract is fine, unless a vanilla bean is specified
veg	vegetable(s)	any non-leafy fresh vegetable that is edible raw, unless otherwise specified
vinegr	vinegar	use plain white or white wine vinegar, unless specified; cider, red, rice, and balsamic vinegar are called for by name
w	with	
walnt	walnut	toast for best flavor; chopped, if not otherwise specified
whip(d)	whip(ped)	to beat vigorously to soft peaks, as with cream or egg whites
whl	whole	
wht	wheat	

TERM	TRANSLATION	MEANING
whtflr	whole wheat flour	
whtgerm	wheat germ	
wk	week(s)	
worces	Worcester-shire sauce	
wrap	wrap in cling film	closely wrapped in plastic cling film unless other material indicated (e.g. foil, pastry)
wt	white	
x	times	the number of times to repeat a step, such as layering or turning
yeast	yeast	active dry yeast, unless otherwise noted
yld	yields	the output of a recipe; a recipe yields 3 to 4 servings, unless otherwise specified
ylw	yellow	
yolk(s)	egg yolk(s)	from large eggs, unless otherwise noted
zest	finely grated citrus rind	loosely packed, from unwaxed fruit, and without any white pith
zuke	zucchini	medium-sized green, unless otherwise noted

CONVERSION CHARTS

All temperatures and measurements have been rounded to the nearest useful unit.

TEMPERATURES

F°	C°	F°	C°
50	10	375	190
70	21	400	200
300	150	425	220
325	160	450	230
350	175	500	260

VOLUMES

American	Imperial	Metric
t (1 teaspoon)	0.16 fluid ounce	5 milliliters
T (1 tablespoon)	½ fluid ounce	15 milliliters
¼c (quarter cup/ 4 tablespoons)	2 fluid ounces	60 milliliters
½c (half cup/ 8 tablespoons)	4 fluid ounces	125 milliliters

VOLUMES

American	Imperial	Metric
c (1 cup/16 tablespoons)	8 fluid ounces	240 milliliters
2c (2 cups/16 fluid ounces/1 U.S. pint)	16 fluid ounces	scant 500 milliliters
4c (4 cups/1 quart)	32 fluid ounces	1 liter
16c (16 cups/ 1 U.S. gallon)	0.83 Imperial gallon	3¾ liters

SPECIAL VOLUMES (FOR BUTTER/SUGAR/FLOUR)

	US/UK	Metric
Butter	c (1 cup/2 sticks/ ½ pound)	225 grams
Sugar	c (1 cup/½ pound/ 6.4 dry ounces)	180 grams
Flour	c (1 cup/⅓ pound/ 5 dry ounces)	140 grams

LENGTHS

American	Metric
⅛" (eighth inch)	3 millimeters
¼" (quarter inch)	6 millimeters
½" (half inch)	1.25 centimeters
1" (one inch)	2.5 centimeters
6" (six inches)	15 centimeters
12" (twelve inches/1 foot)	30 centimeters

WEIGHTS

US/UK	Metric
1oz (1 dry ounce)	scant 30 grams
¼lb (quarter pound/ 4 dry ounces)	115 grams
½lb (half pound/8 dry ounces)	225 grams
lb (1 pound/16 dry ounces)	450 grams

PAN, CAN & JAR MEASUREMENTS

	Translation	American	Metric
8oz jar	eight-ounce jar	1 cup	240 milliliters
bkgdish	standard baking or casserole dish	9 by 13 inches	23 by 33 centimeters
bkgsheet	standard baking or cookie sheet	12 by 15 inches	30 by 38 centimeters
cakepan (or sq pan)	standard cake pan	8 inches diameter	20 centimeters (sub sqpan)
can	regular can*	10½ liquid ounces	310 milliliters
lrgcan	large can*	16 liquid ounces	473 milliliters
loafpan	standard loaf pan	9 by 5 inches	23 by 13 centimeters
pieplate	standard pie plate	9 inches diameter	23 centimeters
qt dish	standard quart or soufflé dish	4 cups	1 liter
ramekin	standard small ramekin	3 inches diameter	7.5 centimeters
skillet	standard skillet	12 inches diameter	30 centimeters

*Refers to the most standard size available

MENUS

These are all-out spreads that include some of my favorite dishes from the book, but they are just suggestions. Compose your menus according to your own tastes.

BREAKFAST IN BED

(COFFEE OR TEA)
Hot Papaya Smoothie (PAGE 75)
Fruit-Baked French Toast
 (PAGE 71)
Mock Clotted Cream with
 lemon zest (PAGE 21)
Coffee Ice Cream (PAGE 199)

LATIN BRUNCH

(COFFEE OR TEA)
Cinnamon Knots (PAGE 54)
Migas (PAGE 73) & Salsa Verde
 (PAGE 100)
Home Fries (PAGE 69)
Fruit Salad (whichever one is
 in season) (PAGE 74)

SPRING

(SAUVIGNON BLANC)
Nettle Soup (PAGE 85)
Green Ravioli (PAGE 142) with
 Spring Mix (PAGE 117)
Manchego Lamb Chops
 (PAGE 159)
Salt Potatoes (PAGE 118)
Tartare de Fraises (PAGE 100)
Rhubarb Upside-Down
 Cupcakes (PAGE 197)

DANISH SPREAD

(PINOT GRIS)

Radishes with Butter & Salt
  (PAGE 105)
Asparagus Soup (PAGE 80)
Prune Pork (PAGE 162) with
  Prune Pork Gravy (PAGE 162)
Mormor's Potatoes (PAGE 118)
Red Slaw (PAGE 92)
Lise's Lemon Mousse (PAGE 181)

THAI-INSPIRED

(SEMILLON)

Almond-Crusted Tofu (PAGE 105)
  with Coconut Sauce (PAGE 37)
Pumpkin Soup (PAGE 86) with
  Sticky Rice (PAGE 125)
Yam Khao Pot (PAGE 93)
Cilantro Prawn Noodles
  (PAGE 137)
Banana Fritters (PAGE 181) with
  Mango Sorbet (PAGE 199)
Spiced Milk Tea (cold) (PAGE 205)

NOUVELLE CUISINE ET CLASSIQUE

(PINOT NOIR)

Maple Lemon Artichokes
  (PAGE 109)
Baked Brie (PAGE 102) with
  Vanilla Zucchini Relish
  (PAGE 25)
Celeriac Velouté (PAGE 82)
Julia Child's Boeuf
  Bourguignon (PAGE 169)
Julia Child's Mushroom &
  Onion Boeuf Garnish (PAGE 169)
Wine Sorbet (PAGE 199)
Midnight Cake (PAGE 194) with
  Lavender Buttercream Icing
  (PAGE 191)

SUMMER

(MINT JULEPS)

Stuffed Zucchini Blossoms
  (PAGE 106)
Melon & Blackberry Soup
  (PAGE 79)
Biftek à la Parrilla (PAGE 161)
Bread Salad (PAGE 91)
Augusta's Blueberry Tart
  (PAGE 189)

INDIAN-FRUIT FUSION
(GEWÜRZTRAMINER)

Pear Chutney (PAGE 24) with
  pappadam
Cauliflower Bites (PAGE 102)
  with Raita (PAGE 99)
Paneer (PAGE 22) in Red Dal
  (PAGE 129)
Vikram Vij's Lamb Chops (PAGE
  159) with Vikram Vij's
  Fenugreek Curry (PAGE 38)
Strawberry Rasam (PAGE 87)
Shortbread (PAGE 170)

MID-SUMMER SPANISH
(SANGRIA)

Alcachofas Fritas with sea salt
  & lemon (PAGE 101)
Pimientos de Padrón (PAGE 101)
Espinacas con Garbanzos
  (PAGE 131)
Gazpacho (PAGE 79)
Paella (PAGE 126)
Flan (PAGE 183)

ITALIAN PRIMO A DIGESTIVO
(SANGIOVESE)

Eggplant Antipasto (PAGE 103)
Minestra di Verdure (PAGE 84)
Fettucine Alfredo (PAGE 139)
Tuscan Pork (PAGE 162)
Composed Tomato Salad
  (PAGE 95)
Tiramisu (PAGE 185)
Limoncello (PAGE 204)

AUTUMN
(BEAUJOLAIS NOUVEAU)

@Blaine's Pear & Spinach
  Pear Soup (PAGE 87)
Endive Risotto (PAGE 127)
Chicken Roulade (PAGE 154)
Broiled Salad (PAGE 91)
Persimmon Pudding (PAGE 184)

NORTHERN FARE

(GOLDEN LAGER)

Mushroom Strudel (PAGE 60)

Irene's Borscht (PAGE 81) with
Crème Fraîche (PAGE 22) and
Soda Rye (PAGE 49)

Scalloped Potatoes (PAGE 120)

Maple Salmon (PAGE 150) with
Linda's Beet Greens (PAGE 112)

Butter Tarts (PAGE 189)

THANKSGIVING

(CHARDONNAY AND SYRAH)

Quinoa Salad (PAGE 95)

Cream-Braised Brussels
Sprouts (PAGE 112)

Roast Turkey (PAGE 157) with
Harvest Stuffing (PAGE 157)
and Fancy Gravy (PAGE 38)

Mashed Potatoes (PAGE 120)

Cranberry Sauce (PAGE 26)

Pumpkin Pie (PAGE 188) with
Honey Ice Cream (PAGE 198)

WINTER

(MULLED CIDER)

Black Pepper Chowder
(PAGE 82) and Sourdough
Bread (PAGE 55)

Skillet Chicken (PAGE 154) with
Chocolate Rosemary Sauce
(PAGE 154)

@Kellan's Fennel &
Pomegranate Salad (PAGE 93)

Butterscotch Pudding
(PAGE 183)

HEARTY IRISH TEATIME

(STRONG BLACK TEA)

Colcannon (PAGE 120)

Guinness Stew (PAGE 170)
with Cheddar Dumplings
(PAGE 168)

Soda Bread (PAGE 49) with
Butter (PAGE 21)

Raw Kale Salad (PAGE 94)

Oatmeal Cookies (PAGE 177)

Hot Toddy (PAGE 207)

MOROCCAN NIGHTS

(HOT GREEN TEA WITH
MINT AND SUGAR)
Kesra flatbread (PAGE 55)
Betzels (PAGE 60) with Basic
  Boiled Egg (PAGE 64) and mint
Bissara (PAGE 81)
Honey Tagine (PAGE 171)
Harissa (PAGE 27) and Couscous
  (PAGE 128)
Orange Watercress Salad
  (PAGE 94)
Coffee-Steeped Dates (PAGE 180)

SUNDAY ROAST DINNER

(GIN & TONIC)
Darjeeling Soup (PAGE 83)
Prime Rib Roast (PAGE 163)
Horseradish Cream (PAGE 24)
Yorkshire Pudding (PAGE 164)
Sweet Carrots (PAGE 113)
Juniper Cabbage (PAGE 113)
Raspberry Fool (PAGE 183)

HORS D'OEUVRES SPREAD

(SPARKLING WINE AND
COCKTAILS TO ORDER)
Gem's Wine-Baked Olives
  (PAGE 103)
Gorgonzola Crostini (PAGE 103)
Vegetable Pâté (PAGE 106)
Melitzanosalata (PAGE 99) with
  pita
Baked Proscuitto & Asparagus
  (PAGE 104)
Cold Avocado Soup (PAGE 78) in
  demitasses
Julia Child's Moules Marinées
  (PAGE 150)
Olive-Oil Cookies (PAGE 178)
  with Basil Ice Cream
  (PAGE 199)

BIBLIOGRAPHY

These are some of the cookbooks on my shelves at home; each is a winner. I may not like following recipes to the letter, but I do enjoy reading them.

Alexiadou, Vefa. *Vefa's Kitchen: The Bible of Authentic Greek Cooking*. London: Phaidon, 2009.

Alford, Jeremy, and Naomi Duguid. *Beyond the Great Wall: Recipes and Travels in the Other China*. New York: Artisan, 2008.

Alford, Jeremy, and Naomi Duguid. *Flatbreads & Flavors*. New York: William Morrow, 1995.

Alford, Jeremy, and Naomi Duguid. *Home Baking: The Artful Mix of Flour and Tradition Around the World*. New York: Artisan, 2003.

Alford, Jeremy, and Naomi Duguid. *Hot Sour Salty Sweet: A Culinary Journey Through Southeast Asia*. New York: Artisan, 2000.

Alford, Jeremy, and Naomi Duguid. *Mangoes & Curry Leaves: Culinary Travels Through the Great Subcontinent*. New York: Artisan, 2005.

Alford, Jeremy, and Naomi Duguid. *Seductions of Rice*. New York: Artisan, 1998.

Bittman, Mark. *How to Cook Everything*. 2nd ed. Hoboken: Wiley, 2008.

Child, Julia, Simone Beck, and Louisette Bertholle. *Mastering the Art of French Cooking.* Vols. 1–2. New York: Knopf, 1961–1970.

Clark, Samantha, and Samuel Clark. *Moro: The Cookbook.* London: Ebury, 2003.

Cresswell, Stephen. *Homemade Root Beer, Soda & Pop.* North Adams, MA: Storey, 1998.

Davidson, Alan *The Oxford Companion to Food.* 2nd ed. Oxford: University Press, 2006.

Davies, Joy. *Noodles and Pasta.* Alexandria, VA: Time Life, 1999.

Dhalwala, Meeru, and Vikram Vij. *Vij's Elegant & Inspired Indian Cuisine.* Vancouver: Douglas & McIntyre, 2006.

Dunlop, Fuchia. *Land of Plenty: A Treasury of Authentic Sichuan Cooking.* London: Penguin, 2003.

Editors of Phaidon Press. *The Silver Spoon: The Bible of Authentic Italian Cooking.* London: Phaidon, 2005.

Editors of Phaidon Press. *The Silver Spoon: Pasta.* London: Phaidon, 2009.

Fulton, Margaret. *Encyclopedia of Food & Cookery.* 2nd ed. Prahran, Australia: Hardie Grant, 2005.

Galvin, Lori, ed. *The New Best Recipe by the Editors of Cook's Illustrated.* 2nd ed. Brookline, MA: America's Test Kitchen, 2004.

Goodman, Myra. *Food to Live By.* New York: Workman, 2007.

Hall Foose, Martha. *Screen Doors and Sweet Tea: Recipes and Tales from a Southern Cook.* New York: Clarkson Potter, 2008.

Katzen, Mollie. *The Moosewood Cookbook.* Berkeley: Ten Speed Press, 1992.

Kurihara, Harumi. *Harumi's Japanese Cooking.* London: Conran-Octopus, 2004.

Larousse Gastronomique. London: Hamlyn, 2009.

Lin, Hsiang Ju, and Tsuifeng Lin. *Chinese Gastronomy.* New York: Harcourt, 1969.

Madison, Deborah. *Vegetarian Cooking for Everyone*. New York: Broadway Books, 1997.

Marks, Gil. *Olive Trees and Honey: A Treasury of Vegetarian Recipes from Jewish Communities Around the World*. Hoboken: Wiley, 2005.

Martin, Guy. *Légumes*. Paris: Chêne-Hachette, 2000.

McGee, Harold. *On Food & Cooking: The Science and Lore of the Kitchen*. London: Hodder & Stoughton, 2004.

Mendel, Janet. *Traditional Spanish Cooking*. Reading, UK: Garnet, 1996.

Morse, Kitty. *North Africa: The Vegetarian Table*. San Francisco: Chronicle Books, 1996.

Novas, Himilce, and Rosemary Silva. *Latin American Cooking Across the USA*. New York: Knopf, 2001.

Ortega, Simone, and Ines Ortega. *1080 Recipes: The Bible of Authentic Spanish Cooking*. London: Phaidon, 2007.

Paré, Jean. *Salads*. 3rd ed. Edmonton: Company's Coming, 1985.

Pellman Good, Phyllis. *The Best of Amish Cooking*. Intercourse, PA: Good Books, 1996.

Peterson, James. *Vegetables*. New York: William Morrow, 1998.

Royo, Koldo. *Tapas y Pintxos de Barcelona*. Barcelona: Styria, 2009.

Russell, Jane. *Irish Farmhouse Cheese Recipes*. Dromore, Ireland: Sommerville Press, 2004.

Schneider, Sally. *A New Way to Cook*. New York: Artisan, 2001.

Shaw, Diana. *Sweet Basil, Garlic, Tomatoes and Chives: The Vegetable Dishes of Tuscany and Provence*. New York: Harmony, 1992.

Tanis, David. *A Platter of Figs*. New York: Artisan, 2008.

Thomas, Anna. *The Vegetarian Epicure*. Vol. 1–2. New York: Random House, 1972–1979.

Xayavong, Daovone. *Taste of Laos*. Berkeley: SLG Books, 2000.

Yagihashi, Takashi. *Takashi's Noodles*. Berkeley: Ten Speed, 2009.

ACKNOWLEDGMENTS

No number of characters is enough to thank the people who have made this cookbook possible.

My respect goes out to everyone at Artisan Books: in particular, to Ingrid Abramovitch, for her guidance and encouragement; Judy Pray and Kathy Brennan, for their spoon-bending faculties in editing this book; Jan Derevjanik, for its superb design; and Ann Bramson, for making it possible.

I am also grateful to my family for their encouragement, teaching, love, and recipes: Kathleen and Mike Evans, my parents; and the extended Cook family, especially Rhoda and Rick Cook. Finally, to my best friend, literary advisor, life partner, and vade mecum, Blaine Cook, for love through all my writing endeavors—thank you so much.

To the teachers who have inspired and encouraged me to write, to imagine, and to create change, you have my gratitude: Keith Maillard, Ian Sansom, Patrick Moore, Matthew Webster, Richard Holmes, and John Lancaster.

Fondest thanks to my friends of pens and feasts—Vanessa Merina, David Lawrence, Irene Barnard, Jean Bertelsen, Morgan Johnson, Riley Hoffman—of the Bay Area every-other-Wednesday writers' group. And to all my friends who insist on inspiration in the kitchen and in life: Aaron Straup Cope, Micholo Grossman, Christi Weindorf, Tom Carden,

Clay Rivers, Gem Spear, Michal Migurski, Judy Hisamatsu, Kellan Elliott-McCrea, Maren Friesen, Margery Simkin, Margot Brennan, Michelle and Jung-Hee Kim, Mollie Copans, Richard Irvine, Sabina Iseli-Otto, Steffen and Lise Norgren, and Yoko Kondo.

Of course, this book was only possible because of the fantastic community that's formed around @cookbook, comprised of so many different people in a day-to-day conversation about food. To each and every person who has taken the trouble to @reply, test, discuss, recommend, or otherwise tweet about my tiny recipes—from the bottom of my heart, thank you for helping me write this book.

INDEX